SECRETS OF SUCCESSFUL RETREATS

The Best From The Non-Profit Pros

D1472259

COMPILED AND EDITED BY

CAROL WEISMAN

SECRETS OF SUCCESSFUL RETREATS
The Best From The Non-Profit Pros

COMPILED AND EDITED BY
CAROL WEISMAN

Published by

F. E. Robbins & Sons Press
St. Louis, Missouri

Preface

My husband and I took our 16-year-old nephew Jake Weisman for a day of water skiing at our friends Pat and Mike Wolff's cabin. Jake was amazed at the level of the general conversation. On the way home, Jake recited conversation after conversation. I told him that the secret of my success is that my friends are all smarter than I am.

I want to thank my friends, clients and colleagues who have taught me so much about the art, craft and science of facilitating a great retreat.

As always, thanks to my mastermind group, Karyn Buxman, Linda Nash, Steve Epner, Sam Silverstein, Lois Creamer and Tony Ruesing. You can't do 40-50 retreats a year without a few bombs. You are always there to help with the post-mortem so that I won't make the same mistake twice.

I have the opportunity to work with Tom Bakewell on several retreats. What a joy! Tom, you are one of the most strategic thinkers I've ever met. Every wild, uncivilized, and at time undisciplined female consultant needs a brilliant, deeply religious Christian gent to whine to, to learn from and to bounce ideas off of. Thanks for all you've taught me.

And now on to my clients: I learned about discussing incredibly difficult issues with respect, passion and kindness from Nancy Murphy and Katie Bannister at the Delta Center for Independent Living.

A special thanks to Josetta Hawthorne and Barbara Price at the Council for Environmental Education. You taught me about how rapidly a board can change when you bring in a brilliant, experienced, female corporate leader.

I have never seen a group implement a plan faster than Schuyler Andrews and Michael Weisbrod at Craft Alliance Gallery. When I returned for a follow-up meeting just six months after your retreat, there had been a spectacular orientation program and many other governance changes instituted. Making changes in many nonprofits is like parallel parking the QE2. You function like a cross between a speed board and the Little Engine that Could.

I learned about courage and tenacity and commitment from Jack Downs, a man living with AIDS. Despite feeling weak and ill and needing a walker, Jack not only got out of bed to attend the Central Illinois Friends of People with AIDS retreat, but he stopped to get cookies to share with the group. Jack, you are an inspiration to all who know you.

Remember the guy on TV years ago who did the commercial about loving the razor so much, he bought the company? The same thing happened to me with the Sequoia National Park Foundation. I fell in love with the magic of the Park and the commitment of the people and was fortunate enough to join. Thanks Sonia Shepard McCellan, Marilyn Riegel, Rod Shepard, Mike Chrisman, Everett Welch, Kay Truesdale, Linda Teter and all the rest of the board and staff for making me feel so welcome.

And last, but never, ever least: Thank you to Frank Robbins, my husband, my friend and my cheerleader. Thank you for taking care of Little Carol when I've been on the road, mailing case after case of books and let us not forget one of our favorite activities: depositing checks in the bank!

Dedication

This book is dedicated to Jack Downs, a man living with AIDS. Despite feeling weak and miserable and ill and barely able to walk, Jack had the commitment and tenacity to attend and actively participate in the retreat for the Central Illinois Friends of People with AIDS. Jack, you're my hero.

Table of Contents

THE GOAL OF AN ICE BREAKER
IS TO BRING THE GROUP CLOSER TOGETHER,
NOT CAUSE A RIOT!

CHAPTER 1

Retreats – Creating an Environment for Success

Steve Epner, BS, CSP

Introduction

Meetings and retreats are used for many different purposes. Sometimes they are to inform a group about decisions that have been made. Other times they are used to develop the strategic or tactical questions that must be answered prior to announcing results internally or to the public.

Environment is often ignored for regular Board meeting, but without great harm. Just about any reasonable meeting space can be made to work. A RETREAT, where the discussion will be longer, more spirited (a nice way to say argumentative) and have serious long-term consequences for the organization is where control of the environment is important.

The environment includes all of the factors around the physical setting of the meeting. It can also include general rules of the meeting. These help set the tone and can greatly influence the results.

We are social animals. Getting together is important any time we have to work out differences, resolve issues or attempt to look into the future. Our meetings can succeed or fail for a large number of reasons. The objective here is to eliminate the environment as a cause of failure.

As with any prescriptive advice, there is always a caveat. When dealing with human beings, there are few absolute answers. If you are uncomfortable with any aspect of the following recommendation, change it. This is not an all or nothing set of suggestions. Use what makes sense to you, the group, the situation and your budget.

Setting up an environment for success may not be difficult, but it is vitally important. While none of the following suggestions are very involved, it takes time and money to do them all. Some meetings are held at the last minute and some groups will have little or no leeway on where to meet or how much money can be spent. Not every aspect of the perfect meeting can be done every time. Do what you can. These ideas work.

Circumstances and budgets have forced all of us to hold meetings in less than ideal circumstances. A poor environment may add a level of complexity and make the facilitator's job more difficult. It does not make it impossible. Just remember, small changes to the environment can have a big impact on the retreat. Do what you can and take advantage of the easy ideas.

Location

The meeting location sets the stage for everything that will come after. Therefore, the first order of business is to determine where to hold the meeting. The choices are really very few. There is a meeting room at someone's office, a restaurant, a hotel, a volunteer's house or a donated space in the basement of some building. It can be at a church or temple, a school or the local community center. It can be in town, in another city or out in the country. Each type of location offers advantages, disadvantages and various levels of cost. If your agency/organization is lucky enough to have sufficient space, that may be your best and least expensive option.

Location also brings up the issue of "come alone" or with a partner or even the whole family. Inviting guests adds an additional level of complexity. Are guests invited to meals or other functions (which will change the dynamics)? How to handle an irate "Other" who is unhappy at being ignored and causes the attendee to lose focus? What if the discussion is going especially well, does it have to be stopped due to scheduling of the guests?

If this is a business meeting for a critical purpose (not all meetings demand full attention), do it without extra attendees. Do not invite guests if there are contentious issues to be resolved. Meetings of general announcements, presentations of project results and where there is little or no dissent are often treated as board member perks. Others should be encouraged to attend. It is a chance to get away and can be a major benefit to the attendee and their guest or family.

An office, for all of its positives, may not be the best choice. It is frequently the least expensive, but is prone to interruptions by phone calls, people who just happen to drop by and that sudden emergency, "…as long as you are here, can you take just a second to…."

If a member of the Board or committee donates the office space, be careful of "taking advantage" of your special friends. Where possible, at least offer to pay for the cost of food and beverages, provide clean up assistance and thank any support staff at the office who help the meeting run smoothly.

The seating and setting of the work area is the next consideration. Again, for a regular board meeting that is to approve previous action, where there is little contention and there is general agreement on the actions to take, any table in any location can work.

Restaurants are OK for shorter meetings and working meals. Their "party" rooms are not always conducive to contentious retreats. The chairs tend to be harder, the spaces less sound proof (i.e. you can be disturbed by groups next door) and the lighting is dimmer.

Meetings in restaurants are not known for having lots of workspace. If you expect people to be taking notes, shuffling stacks of paper or needing to spread out, there are better environments. This does not mean that a meal in a restaurant at a hotel setting will not work, just plan to use it for a discussion topic where one person per group or table can be appointed to take notes. Then review what was discovered when you reconvene.

Check the space out for "quietness." Wherever possible, insist on an empty room between you and the nearest activity or other meeting. Do not accept rooms near a live band or D.J. Be especially careful of large group meetings near by. They often tend to be loud and will interfere with what you are doing.

Hotels and resorts normally provide the best meeting options, but are usually the most expensive. They are flexible in terms of furniture, room arrangement and special setups. One organization can arrange for your meals, beverages and overnight services for multi-day retreats. Do not reject this option out of hand. You may be surprised at the special deals you can get, especially at a city/business location over a weekend.

Be careful of fancy resorts, these can sometimes confuse the focus of the meeting. If everyone is chomping at the bit to get out to a famous golf course, they will not be concentrating on the business of the organization. Once again, know your group and their desires. Some high power boards are willing to pay extra to attend a meeting where they can get some much deserved "R&R" and even bring their family.

There are exceptions to every rule, but for most non-profit meetings, the location needs to be easy and convenient to get to. If your attendees are flying in, facilities near airports with free transportation are always winners. Pick airports that most of the participants can get to non-stop.

If you use a city location, pick it for convenience as well. Make sure to arrange for parking in advance. Most board members do not like surprises. An unexpected $15 parking tab may not be a financial burden for the big donors, but it could become an irritant and a reason that leads to an important volunteer dropping off the board. For an underpaid (or unpaid) volunteer, it may create an embarrassment if they do not have the cash to get out of the parking garage.

Always make an in person visit to any site. Pictures and brochures do not tell the real story. See the room you will meet in, see where you will eat and, if overnight accommodations are to be used, see the rooms. Check for ADA compliance especially if you know attendees will be using wheelchairs or need other assistance. It is your responsibility to make sure everything is top notch and works for your group.

The Room

The room itself needs to be large enough for comfort and have room to "move." Oddly shaped rooms may look good in the pictures, but seldom work as well as a traditional square or rectangle. When there are less than eight people, almost any board type room with an oval or rectangular table will work. Groups of over twenty require many special arrangements (and are beyond the scope of this chapter). The following guidelines will work best for groups between eight and twenty.

Our experience suggests that thirty linear inches is a reasonable amount of space per person at a table. Therefore, eight people (four on a side) need a table at least ten feet long. This may seem large, but if you are going to be sitting there for eight to ten hours, the space is necessary. Twenty-four inches is the minimum to be able to do anything. It is not as comfortable, provides little "personal space" and certainly will not be conducive to a tough meeting agenda.

Space is necessary between the sides of the table and the walls so people can move around. A good minimum is three feet from the table to the nearest wall. That way, someone can squeeze behind a participant sitting at the table.

If there is space, a coffee break service in the room is a wonderful perk. The longer the meeting, the more necessary it is. There should be space to stand at the coffee service without interfering with any participant. Some meeting rooms have a service bar built in. These take up less meeting space and are very effective.

At the front of the room, space for a facilitator to work and write on easels requires five to six feet in front of the table. The facilitator will often have a chair for meals, but it is usually pushed under the table or kept out of the way during most of the meeting.

When setting the room, windows and doors can be a problem. The best setup is for the door to be at the back of the room. That way, attendees can enter and leave without interfering with the facilitator or disturbing the meeting (or at least minimizing the disturbance that will be caused).

Windows should also be at the back of the room or have drapes / shades that can be pulled. There is nothing worse than a meeting where the participants are looking out on a sunny day with a beach or mountains in the view. Their attention will constantly be a million miles away. Uncovered windows at the front of the room are to be avoided at all costs. No one can look at a "back lit" facilitator for very long.

The temperature of the room will never be right for everyone. A simple rule of thumb, it is always better a bit cooler than hotter. Most of us can add a sweater if we get a little chilled (I am not talking about keeping the thermostat at 40 degrees), but there is a limit to what we can remove if it gets too warm. Plus warm encourages sleep.

If you have a thermostat in the room, put one person in control. If everyone is jumping up to swing the setting from one extreme to the other, you end up with anarchy and a very uncomfortable, distracted meeting.

Lighting is the other variable that makes a big difference. Bright light keeps everyone more awake and alert. If your presentations require a projector, get one that works in full light. Where you need to dim the light to see a projected image, try to turn off (or unscrew the light bulbs) that are right above the screen. That way, the working space is still well lit. Remember, dimmed lights (like too warm a temperature) encourage sleep.

Should there be a clock in the room? Since just about everyone will have a watch, you are not going to keep the time a secret. However, the preference is to have the clock, if there is one, in the back of the room. It becomes the official clock and can be used for timing specific discussions or to determine penalties for late returns from breaks.

(One way I get everyone back on time after a break or meal is to set the expectation based on the official clock – my watch if there is no clock in the room; I always pick an odd time like 17 after – it is easier to remember; Then, if anyone is late, they have to tell a joke to the rest of the group; Not a big penalty, but one that seems to work.)

Set Up

The actual set up of the meeting space will affect the levels and types of interaction. In a small group, keep everyone close. For three to six, small round tables work. Six to nine people can meet at a boardroom table. For groups over ten (and even for some groups as small as eight) the "U" or horseshoe shape is the most effective. There is more room to spread out, the seating is more flexible and facilitating the meeting is easier. A meeting of twenty people can be easily managed with this setup.

No matter which configuration you use, be very careful with where people sit. If there is a divisive issue to be discussed, do not allow the participants to create "us and them" seating. This will immediately set up confrontation and is to be avoided at all costs. Assign seats so that the "sides" will be mixed up. It forces conversation and reduces rancor. (See the next section on Seating Assignments for a more detailed review of the issues and suggestions.)

Whenever possible use tables that are thirty inches deep. The extra room is worthwhile and provides sufficient space for food, drink, notes and even a laptop computer. Provide enough room for the facilitator to move comfortably in the middle of the "U." Good facilitators know how to use this space to defuse conflict and to encourage discussion.

In some situations, where there will be significant time set aside for work by smaller groups or committees, the use of "3/4 rounds" makes sense. Set up round tables where seating is only provided around three quarters of the table. Plan on four to six persons per table. That way, everyone can be set facing the front, but they are ready for individual discussions or working breakouts.

Try to not use tables normally set for ten or twelve people. Participants are too far apart for a workgroup. They have to yell to be heard and either disturb the rest of the room, or just drop out of the conversation. When using rounds, the seating rules below still apply.

The chairs should be as comfortable as possible. Chairs on wheels, which can tilt, have a height adjustment and can swivel are best. Inexpensive stacking chairs do not work as well. They are uncomfortable and increase fatigue just when you need everyone's fullest attention. If folding chairs are the only option, include more frequent breaks. If at all possible, give participants a reason or permission to move around the space and stretch.

Some facilities can provide a sofa or two in the room. These work best in small informal groups where the ability to be more comfortable and to change one's location improve the conversation. The larger the group and the more formal the meeting, the less positive value will be added.

Seating Assignments

Probably the most overlooked environmental aspect of the meeting is assigned seating. Most meetings allow random seating based on "first come, first served." This mentality leaves your meeting's success to chance. People will select their seats by cliques and egocentric arrangements that can reduce communication and encourage factionalism.

In advance of the meeting, establish the seating charts. Do not leave it to chance. There are a few simple rules that will improve the meeting. First, separate people who work together or are "best friends." This will minimize side conversations. Next, intermingle ranks and reporting relationships. If there are "sides," make sure they are interspersed. Keep power players separate.

Then recognize that specific seats have differing amounts of power associated with them (see Figure 1). Put your most powerful attendees in the weakest seats. It allows the facilitator to control their contribution as opposed to fighting against them if they attempt to overwhelm the meeting. By the same token, the strong seats help your shy or less vocal participants be heard. It is easier to draw out their ideas and comments.

If there will be working meals in a separate room, then arrange seating for that location as well. The same types of rules may apply. Any time you want to have open discussion or idea generation, mixing people up encourages new input and viewpoints. If you need

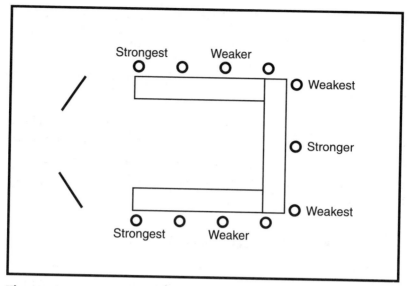

Figure 1

to make decisions or want to take specific actions, then grouping people by department, responsibility or rank may be appropriate.

Set the room with name tents so everyone will know where they are to sit. Tents can be made out of any paper, but a heavier, card stock is better. You can hand print the first names in large letters or let a computer print the names in 70-point type. This is the easiest way to get people to go where you want them. Always bring a couple of blanks and a large marker pen for the inevitable correction, new person or unexpected guest.

Name tents have the added advantage of helping the facilitator remember names. If your group meets infrequently or has many new faces, name tents help everyone get to know each other. By including the name on the back of the tent, it will help each person's neighbor to remember names as well.

Use special markings (Group A, B or C; Meal table 1, 2 or 3) on the inside of the tent to indicate where each person is to sit for breakouts, meals or other functions. Then have identifiers that match the codes on the tables to be used. This is an easy way to control the groups for breakout sessions and to encourage "mingling" during meals.

Timing

Time is so very important in our busy lives. Time away from work can be intimidating to some, loathed by workaholics and considered a vacation by others. A small amount of consideration will go a long way to increase the effectiveness of any meeting.

To begin with, Monday mornings are tough for many people. They want to be able to get their teams started for the week and catch up on the weekend activities before being out of the office for a full day or more. If they are flying in, missing Sunday dinner with the family is another imposition that may not be appreciated. Friday afternoons are another time to avoid. The mind leaves for the weekend long before the body can join. Use these days only in conjunction with a weekend retreat.

Weekends themselves offer unique possibilities for non-profit groups. It may be easier for the businessperson to give the meeting their fullest attention. If the meeting is planned far enough in advance, it is possible for the individual to plan other activities around the meeting schedule.

Where possible, start morning meetings before the business day begins. Any meeting that starts after the beginning of the day will start late. It is almost an unwritten rule of life. If you give busy people the opportunity to go to their desks before going to the meeting, something will delay them – guaranteed. Start with a light breakfast for the early risers and to give them a reason to miss traffic if driving to the meeting location. Do not start the meeting later than 8:00 a.m. if you want to begin on time.

Lunch is another good starting time. It is a natural break time in the day and people will usually find they can leave to get to your meeting on time. Call the lunch for 11:30 and beat the lunchtime traffic. The actual meeting may not start until 1:00, but by then everyone (even the "always late" people) will be there and ready to go.

3:00 or 3:30 is the best afternoon time, especially if you will meet into the evening. It gives everyone time to get most of their work done for the day and still avoid rush hour traffic to get to the meeting location. If people are flying in, it saves an extra overnight away from home and allows all but the West Coast to East Coast flyers to get there easily on the same day. Just like lunch, start with a coffee/cookie break so there is a buffer to reward the "on-timers" while waiting for the later arrivals.

Even though you have set a time, what do you do when some are late? One thing is to set up a penalty in advance. Having to tell a joke works. Also a donation to the organization is a good idea. The big question is: when do you really start? What if the head of the committee is late? What do you do? Waste everyone's time while you wait for the leader to show up or try to start the meeting missing the most important participant?

The easiest way to solve this problem is to not appoint chairs who are always late. Now that you have had a good laugh, consider having all of the material to be distributed in YOUR hands in advance. That way you can hand the material out to be read while waiting (of course, you have sent this material to everyone in advance, but we all know few if any will read it and even fewer will remember to bring it with them).

Next, be prepared to call the meeting to order and get all of the administriva out of the way. Approve the previous meeting minutes and what ever else can be done without "you-know-who." Then have the non-controversial reports given. When all of the updates are done, the gossip completed and the chair is not there, it is decision time. A decision must be made and is different with each group and meeting. Your two choices are to (1) start the meeting without that person or (2) cancel the meeting and let everyone go home, back to work or to the golf course.

One sneaky way I try to keep from being in that position is to call a special meeting of the leadership just prior to the main retreat getting started. My goal is to have all of the critical ears at the meeting location an hour ahead of the start time for the retreat. If it is an 8:00 a.m. meeting, we will have an executive breakfast at 7. Some people are just always late – work around them as much as possible.

Finally, watch out for holidays, especially the religious kind. Many meetings have become disasters because the date was picked without regard to the tremendous diversity in our volunteers today. The very people who will be offended may not recognize a conflicting date in advance and only at the last minute realize they cannot attend. Then they wonder if you did not care about their participation or are prejudiced against their group. Check the calendar carefully and specifically ask about upcoming celebrations.

Breaks are another important issue. If there are smokers in the group, then breaks may have to be more often and longer or you will lose their input. Normally, a good facilitator will recognize the need for a break and call one as necessary. We normally agree in advance that everyone will break at the same time. Our rule is anyone can request a break and then we all go at once. It minimizes the distractions and keeps everyone in all of the discussions.

A good rule of thumb is that a break should be taken at least every 90 minutes. Ten to fifteen minutes is a reasonable length. If it is longer, you will lose attendees to phone calls and emergencies that they had time to find out about. Where you are on hard chairs or the environment is less than ideal, more frequent stretch breaks are most appreciated by all of the attendees.

Meal breaks are usually thirty to forty five minutes. A working lunch or dinner may last longer, but always allow an extra fifteen minutes after every meal for nature breaks and to move around without the group. Do not serve alcohol at any meal where you will want people to return to the meeting after eating.

Where possible, a coffee / break service should be in the room at all times. Today, it is important to include regular and decaf coffee, regular, diet and decaf soda (soft drinks), regular and decaf tea and bottled water. In the morning provide some type of pastry choice (donuts, pound cake and bread / bagel). An hour or so after lunch, bring out an assortment of cookies (chocolate chip if I am your facilitator) or sweets to raise blood sugar levels. Munchies for meetings after dinner depend on the individuals in the group. Fresh fruit is appreciated all day long.

Meals

A whole book could be written on meals at meetings – and there is a wonderful chapter on the topic in this book. Here are just a few simple suggestions to consider. Begin by surveying (or knowing well) all of the attendees to find their eating preferences. Make sure you know about any special dietary needs (for example: Kosher, Vegetarian, Low salt, etc.).

Next, keep all meals light. Serve a full steak dinner for lunch and watch your attendees sleep most of the afternoon. Sandwich and salad buffets are nice and give everyone a choice of what to eat. Breakfast buffets work as well. Oatmeal is very appreciated by attendees who watch their cholesterol. Juices should include at least one alternative to orange.

If you want to work through meals, consider using that time for discussions. Have each table report back to the group after the meal is done. It is a great break from the meeting routine and encourages people to meet others if you mix up the seating.

Beat the hunger pains if at all possible. That means to serve breakfast as early as people can be expected to arrive. Lunchtime should start between 11:30 and noon. Dinner is appropriate any time after 5:00. If space and the agenda allow, have the meals in a different room. The change of view is invigorating for the mind and helps people perform at their best.

Props

Most retreats require a small number of props to help them run smoothly and to organize the effort. Flip charts are the most used item at any retreat. For most retreats, two easels are best. One is used for keeping notes and the second is an "idea parking lot" to capture great thoughts for later discussion. The second easel also allows you to be prepared if the first one runs out of paper without interrupting the meeting to reload.

There are many types of paper you can use today. Standard sized flip charts are not standard, but can easily be found in 27 by 34 inch pads. Some people prefer to have lines or squares preprinted to make it easier to write straight. Check with the meeting leader or facilitator to find their preference. Then make sure you start with a (relatively) full pad. Keep the "one or two sheets left" pads for use at the office.

Since most flip chart writing ends up on a wall somewhere, either "post it" note type sheets; "static cling" sheets; or masking tape will be necessary. Check with the facility to see if they have rules against using tape on their walls, wallpaper or only painted surfaces.

Also check that the paper is of sufficient weight (thickness). That way, you can write on a sheet already hanging on the wall without leaving a reminder of your visit on the wall behind the sheet. Cleaning wallpaper can be very expensive.

There should be a set of at least three colored and one black marker. The longer the retreat, the more important it is to have spares. If the facility has a white board, be careful not to use permanent markers on their board.

As a quick hint to make life after the meeting easier, number each sheet as you start it in the upper right corner. This makes it easy to get all of the charts in chronological order no matter how many you have used or where they end up on the wall.

Some meetings use electronic white boards so that copies of each chart can be produced (without transcription) for each attendee – while at the meeting. These are nice, but at the end of the meeting, you may not have all of the notes that were added by individuals after a sheet was passed out.

Another prop that has become common in many retreat environments is the "Talk Ball." All too often, our board members like to interrupt or carry on multiple conversations. A simple ball, toy animal or other fun prop can be used to designate who has the floor. Until that item is passed, no one else can speak. It makes it easier for those that need a second to collect their thoughts to finish a statement without worrying that someone else will jump in if there is one half second of silence.

Other toys can be used effectively if there are high levels of tension. People can be given "smiles" on a stick to wave when being facetious. Like an "☺" at the end of an email.

Other

Here are a few final ideas to help the meeting be as successful as possible. Each will improve the environment for thinking and contributing.

First, have all beepers, cell phone and wireless email devices turned off! If someone absolutely needs to be reachable, set the device to vibrate. Ask them to alert their staff and family that they are at an important meeting and are only to be interrupted for a real emergency. Remember, any interruption is an excuse to leave the meeting.

Arrange for the meeting facility to accept calls (if available) and take messages. These can be brought to the room in an emergency. Otherwise, they should be taped outside the door to be picked up at breaks.

Second, all egos and titles are checked at the door. Most retreats depend on sharing of ideas and thoughts. If one or two people are going to be allowed to dictate the answers, then why hold the meeting? Everyone has something to add or you are inviting the wrong people. Inside the room, it has to be a level playing field to get the most value from the attendees.

Third, there is only one conversation at a time. Very few people can keep up with and participate in multiple discussions. And it is impolite to ignore what another person believes to be an intelligent addition to the discussion. Let everyone have his or her say and rely on a professional facilitator to control the time everyone takes.

Fourth, break together. The mood is easily broken if people are constantly getting up and leaving the room. You may even encourage conversations to be held outside the room destroying the advantage of meeting together. Do not lose anyone's participation. When someone needs a break, let them request it. Than everyone goes and returns at the same time. It is then easier to build consensus and a sense of "team."

Fifth, prior to the meeting, send a formal invitation. Include the agenda to be followed, a list of the objectives, all meeting details (include time, location, instructions for parking and where to have messages sent) and any "homework" that is to be done in advance.

Sixth, have pencils, pens and paper for the attendees. It is inconceivable that an otherwise intelligent board member or staffer would come to a meeting unprepared, but it happens all of the time. If reports were distributed in advance for review, have extra copies to hand out onsite.

Finally, provide a report at the conclusion of the meeting. Include copies of flip charts or just a summary of what was accomplished. Know your audience and take care of their needs. This includes all of the people that did not participate but will be affected by the outcome.

Conclusion

Retreats are a valuable means of achieving many ends. Goals, agendas and process are as individual as the organizations, attendees and facilitators. Yet all have to be held in a physical environment. While the best environment in the world will not save a poorly conceived or managed retreat, it can greatly enhance the potential for success.

* * * * *

Steve Epner is a well-known consultant and meeting facilitator. He works with strong, self-confident organizations to find new ways to resolve old problems. Steve creates environments to encourage people to define their visions, plan to achieve objectives and then manage change for success.

Steve Epner, BS, CSP

To know Steve Epner, just take a look at his office. Most offices have "work stations," Steve has "play stations." Among his piles of computer literature and family pictures, are magic tricks and toys of every description and type.

His fascination with all that surrounds him is what makes Steve a sought after consultant, speaker and author. He makes technology simple and the simple magical.

Steve has been directing traffic on the information super highway since 1966. Beginning as an operator in a "tab shop" environment, Steve has progressed through the computer age serving in various roles including operations, programming, system development, project management and general management.

As a consultant, Steve helps bring businesses and technology together. Clients learn to effectively utilize their information resources to help them reach the future. Clients have learned to count on Steve's enviable reputation for working with teams to develop business plans that do not end up collecting dust on a shelf. As president of BSW Consulting, Steve is also known for finding ways to use information as a competitive tool.

Steve understands that technology is valuable only if it solves real business problems. By encouraging active involvement from all levels of management and staff, "project teams" take ownership of decisions, diagnose situations, focus on high priority issues, discover unique solutions and manage for success.

Facilitating strategic and tactical planning meetings for both technical and non-technical groups are among Steve's talents. He is an expert who encourages competing views, while preventing a shouting match. Many sessions include training the client organization to manage future meetings. Steve appears at conferences, shows, and meetings across the country. A highly regarded industry expert, Steve is widely published and has provided comment for national business publications including the *Wall Street Journal*.

Steve is the founder (1976) and past president of the Independent Computer Consultants Association. Steve continues to be active in leading the consulting industry toward goals of professionalism and responsibility to the client community. Steve is a past president of the St. Louis Gateway Chapter of the National Speakers Association.

Steve Epner, CSP
BSW Consulting, Inc.
1050 N. Lindbergh Blvd., St. Louis, MO 63132
314-983-1214 • Fax: 314-983-1329
E-mail: sepner@bswc.com
www.bswc.com

CHAPTER 2

Making the Retreat Experience: Choosing – and Using – Facilitators Wisely

Terrie Temkin, Ph.D.

T he decision was made to go forward with the retreat. Now, all you need is a facilitator – right? Perhaps you should just call the consultant that ran your capital campaign last year...

Well, maybe. A facilitator can make a retreat, or turn it into a disaster. No matter how wonderful that consultant might be, he or she may not be right for your organization – at least at this particular time. It may be that he or she is not the best person for the job at hand. After all, everyone has his or her areas of expertise. It might also be that you cannot afford that person. Important to a productive and memorable retreat experience is knowing what you require of a facilitator and knowing how to ensure that you find someone within your budget who can provide just that.

This chapter was written to help you maximize the experience of choosing and using retreat facilitators. It covers:

- The importance of considering your specific needs.

- The difference between facilitators, trainers and consultants and the services they offer.

- How to determine if you have to go outside the organization for a facilitator.

- How to weigh the benefits of hiring a facilitator against the costs.

- The steps you can take to find the right facilitator once you've made the decision to move ahead, including identifying a pool of potential facilitators and narrowing the field to your top candidates.

- The questions you can ask to better ascertain when you have found the *right* person.

- How to contract with the facilitator so that nothing is left to chance.

- What you should expect from the person you choose.

- How to work with the facilitator for optimum results.

Assessing Your Specific Needs

Spending the time – before you ever pick up a telephone – to assess your desired outcomes, your budget, and what you really want from a facilitator will pay many times over. You will save time and energy because you will only be proceeding in a manner you can afford, and you will only be calling people who truly have the potential to enhance your retreat. You will be able to keep the conversations short and to the point because you will be prepared to state your needs and expectations succinctly as well as to answer the questions the facilitators are most likely to ask of you. And, you will earn the respect and appreciation of your participants when they find that their retreat time is well spent because the facilitator focused directly on the key issues and kept the dialog moving thanks to your direction.

At the very least, answer the following questions before starting your search. The more specific your analysis, the better outcome you can expect

- What is your purpose for holding a retreat?

- What instigated the need for a retreat at this specific point in time?

- What is your retreat budget?

- Who do you expect to invite to the retreat and why?

- What would you like the facilitator to do for you, that is, how are you defining "facilitation"?

- What would you like to be different in your organization as a result of the retreat?

DEFINING YOUR PURPOSE

It seems obvious to say that you have to define your purpose. Unfortunately, facilitators get calls every day from people who have given no thought to this. The callers know they want the facilitator to work with them, but when asked what their goals are the answer is either silence or a request to do whatever the facilitator thinks is best.

There are a myriad of different reasons why an organization might hold a retreat. For instance, it might want the time to work on uniting its team around common goals, reflect on its mission, vision and values, or plan for the future. Perhaps it needs to develop solutions for specific problems, prepare for a major campaign, resolve conflict, or consider possible collaborations. It might want the privacy to evaluate the executive director or the workings of the board. Or, it might want to teach solicitation techniques or educate the participants about the organization, the demographics affecting it, the group's roles and responsibilities, or key issues that are too complex to consider in the course of a typical day, such as legislative issues or legal challenges.

What is *your* reason for holding this retreat? Be as specific as possible when answering this question. Certainly you can approach potential facilitators with a generalized need such as "board development." However, you will find it much easier to zero in on the right facilitator if you can say that you need someone to present the concepts of Duty of Care and Duty of Loyalty to the board.

Besides the fact that most facilitators will want this specificity to design an appropriate retreat day, there is a second reason for clarifying your needs. The reality is that not every facilitator is equally good at facilitating each type of retreat. Most are content experts in one or a few areas. For instance, let us assume that you are contemplating a merger. Any facilitator would probably find it relatively easy to keep the discussion focused on the topic of the merger, especially if your group is excited about the possibilities it perceives. However, if that person fails to understand the issues that must be raised, such as the need for integrating two boards, designing a new organizational chart, and linking two different technology systems, the discussion may be interesting but it most likely will be ineffectual. If you want your retreat to be a success you need a facilitator that knows these issues, as well as where the landmines are usually buried in merger discussions and how to keep both sides at the table when the going gets tough.

IDENTIFYING WHAT IS PROMPTING
THE NEED FOR A RETREAT AT THIS TIME

Obviously, your chances of finding the right facilitator increase with your ability to articulate your needs. For instance, you will gain a better idea of what different facilitators can provide if, instead of merely saying 'people don't work together,' you can list symptoms that lead you to conclude that the organization has conflict issues to resolve. And, if you can state what you believe to be the underlying problem, that is even better. Try to identify such factors as the history behind the issue, the effect you see the symptoms having on the organization's stakeholders, and the consequences you fear if these symptoms are left unchecked.

Of course, policy, procedure or convention may mandate the call for a retreat. Examples of retreats that fall in this category are:

- Annual goal-setting sessions,

- Evaluations of the executive director,

- Self-assessments of the board, or

- Board orientations.

In these situations, communicating the organization's needs to potential facilitators becomes easier as a function of gaining experience with the process. Ultimately, that experience also makes it easier to select the best facilitator for your purposes. Consider a situation where your organization has experimented with a number of different evaluation techniques and has settled on comparing success against previously defined objectives. You can quickly limit your search by weeding out those facilitators who prefer using "off-the-shelf" evaluation tools.

Assessing Your Pocketbook

Retreats can be costly. You may incur expenses for the rental of space and audio-visual equipment, food, special invitations, and materials, as well as a facilitator. Your budget should have a line item for any retreats it expects to hold. A quick review of the monies currently allotted will help you target the range of facilitation services you can afford.

Considering the Invitation List

You should also consider the potential impact of your invitation list on your choice of a facilitator. A heterogeneous group is likely to require a facilitator who is capable of balancing many different opinions. A homogeneous group has to determine if it wants a facilitator who resembles its members or at least has experience with groups similar to it. Such a group also has to determine if it wants a facilitator who will challenge its beliefs or remain neutral.

The size of the group can affect your choice as well. With a large group you might find it advantageous to use a facilitator with large group experience or more than one facilitator.

Defining What You Want the Facilitator to Do for You

What are you hoping the person can accomplish with your group? Do you want someone to create a retreat agenda and facilitate the process, or are you providing the agenda and expecting the facilitator to keep your group on task? Do you expect the facilitator to meet with a number of people prior to the retreat or do you feel you can provide enough information over the phone? Are you looking for someone who will keep a written record of the retreat and give you a report, or are you arranging to have someone else take minutes, transcribe and distribute them? Do you want the person to spend the entire day with your group, even though his or her part is only two hours? You see where this is going. It is important that you clarify what you will expect from a facilitator so that you can communicate those expectations to everyone you interview and settle on the person with the knowledge-base, skills, and level of experience you need most.

IDENTIFYING WHAT YOU HOPE WILL BE DIFFERENT AS A RESULT OF THE RETREAT

Finally, you surely have some expectations regarding what should result from this retreat. Put those expectations into words. Again, be as specific as possible. Define your criteria for success. State those actions or behaviors you hope will be different following the retreat. It will be easier for a facilitator to help you achieve your desired goals if everyone can articulate what those are.

Types of Facilitators

Just as there are different reasons why you might hold a retreat, there are different types of retreat facilitators. Knowing what you would like your facilitator to do for you will help you choose the right type. The three types of facilitators most commonly used for retreats are facilitators, trainers, and organizational development consultants.

Facilitators, in the purest sense, move a process along. If your organization is holding a goal-setting session you would want to hire a facilitator. With his or her specialized knowledge of group dynamics he or she can keep the discussions focused, make sure everyone has a say in decision making, ensure that both the organization's and the individuals' objectives are met, and encourage across-the-board buy-in of the final product.

Trainers are information providers, sharing new or critical ideas, techniques or philosophies to help the organization function at an optimum level. They are skilled at generating learning through a variety of interactive techniques, such as activities, case studies and discussion. Using an earlier example, you would use a trainer to facilitate a board's understanding of its Duties of Care and Loyalty.

Organizational Development Consultants intervene in the organization to improve its efficiency and effectiveness. Generally, they guide an organization through a change process to reach a mutually defined endpoint. They often conduct an organizational audit then recommend changes in form and function. You would want to use an organizational development consultant if you are conducting a strategic plan, for instance.

These different types of facilitators are not necessarily mutually exclusive. One facilitator may play several roles. The key in choosing the right facilitator is finding someone who has the skills, is a good collaborator and who has a style that works well with both the task at hand and the culture of your organization.

Knowing When to Seek Outside Help

The most obvious answer to when you need an outside facilitator is when there is no one in the organization with the skills you need. However, even in situations where you do have someone with the requisite skills you may seriously want to look outside your own organization. Why? There are several reasons.

One of the most important is neutrality. Even though the person within your organization may be able to remain totally professional, allowing all viewpoints equal time, you want to be able to protect that person from any claims of bias. An outside facilitator comes without allegiance to any group or idea and is, therefore, given the benefit of the doubt when closing off conversation to move the process along or mediating between two opposing viewpoints.

Another important reason for bringing in an outside facilitator is getting a fresh perspective. Organizations tend to become insular in their thinking. An outside facilitator who works with a variety of groups often sees potential pitfalls in favored proposals. More importantly, he or she can recommend alternative approaches.

Communicating the importance of the retreat to those you have invited is yet another reason why you might want to use an outside facilitator. When people learn that this is important enough to merit the investment of dollars they are often more appreciative of the need to show up.

Weighing the Benefits Against Costs

Speaking of dollars, you have a fiduciary responsibility to analyze what you expect to gain against your anticipated costs. You can keep the process simple. Generating a pros and cons list should provide you with the information you need. Consider, for instance, how your invitees will feel if the retreat drags on or ends without a sense of accomplishment.

If you will allow some editorializing, while it can be expensive to hire a facilitator, it can be doubly so not to. The attorney and quote meister William Shea, Jr. once said, "When considering an investment, remember that the future is longer than the present."

The Steps to Finding the Right Facilitator

Scenario I

It was the week between Christmas and New Year's. The facilitator was on vacation when she received a call forwarded to her cell phone. The caller explained that someone – he didn't remember who or under what circumstance – gave him the facilitator's name. His organization was planning a three-hour retreat for January 3rd – yes, just a few days away. Would the facilitator be available? The group wanted leadership training. What kind of leadership training, asked the facilitator? Just leadership training – something that would fit in the block of time they were allotting. The caller never did ask the facilitator if she did leadership training.

Scenario II

A woman spoke up at the planning meeting. She knew someone who would probably facilitate the upcoming retreat for free. This person facilitated workshops in his field – construction – for a living. In fact, he was well known and was often called upon to speak all over the country for very large sums of money. The rest of the board quickly agreed to have the woman pursue this wonderful opportunity.

If only the above scenarios were unusual. Unfortunately, they are not. What is even more unfortunate is that these retreats are bound to fail. This is because the planners have neglected the assessment process and there is little or no logical reason for whom they select to facilitate their retreat. The second scenario is also doomed if "free" becomes "costly" because the facilitator doesn't understand nonprofits or is lured out of town by big bucks at the last minute.

IDENTIFYING AN APPROPRIATE POOL OF FACILITATORS

Most consulting jobs today are awarded on the basis of personal relationships. This is true when it comes to choosing retreat facilitators as well. However, while knowing how someone works or liking the person is a plus, you should not consider this sufficient data upon which to make your hiring decision. Having a pool of facilitators from which to choose helps ensure that you will find the right facilitator for the job at hand. To build a facilitator pool, try the following:

- Talk with people who have worked successfully with your organization in the past.

- Ask your board members for the names of facilitators they have seen in action.

- Ask colleagues in the community for the names of facilitators they have used for similar types of retreats, and with whom they were pleased.

- Call the community foundation, technical assistance center or United Way in your area for referrals.

- Depending on the focus of your retreat, contact your local chapter of the Association of Fundraising Professionals, American Society of Association Executives, Directors of Volunteer Services, American Society of Training and Development, Organization Development Network, International Society for Performance and Instruction, or similar professional organization. Many of these organizations have online consultant directories, such as the *Association of Fundraising Professionals Facilitators' Directory* – http://www.afpnet.org – or the *Association of Volunteer Administrators Facilitators' and Trainers' Directory* – http://www.avaintl.org/resources/candt.html.

- Look in the classified sections of such publications as *NonProfit Times* and *The Chronicle of Philanthropy*.

- Check with a local university. Many professors do consulting on the side and have facilitation experience. Others will know of people to recommend.

- Ask your colleagues on one of the many computer bulletin boards designed for sharing information in the nonprofit sector.

- Go online to check out the national online nonprofit consultants' register at http//:www.charitychannel.com/resources/Consultants_Registry_Online/index.html.

- Read the nonprofit literature. You will find people who are writing on relevant topics. Since most journals and newsletters include contact information for their authors, it is an easy task to contact those authors that say what you feel needs to be said.

Narrowing the Field

Unfortunately, far too many organizations narrow the field by considering only price. Fees should be your *last* screen. You've come this far, look first at the degree to which you have a match of skills, knowledge, and experience against the criteria you specified in your initial needs assessment. Look too for a facilitator who can demonstrate a successful track record on similar projects.

To ascertain the above you might request either a brief phone interview or a short – one or two page – summary of their experience and the approach they might take with your group. Follow this with an in-person interview of only the top candidates.

When interviewing, resist the tendency to give a lot of credence to your gut-level impressions. Chemistry is important, but the answers to your key questions are more important. Ask hypothetical questions to determine how each candidate might respond to situations he or she is likely to encounter. In the interview be sure to cover the following:

- The facilitator's experience.

- The ability of the facilitator to listen and to comprehend the issues and their implications.

- The knowledge the facilitator has about your organization, and the level of respect he or she has for the skills and experience of the people in it.

- The facilitator's reputation as someone who is knowledgeable, skilled, reliable and honest.

- The degree to which a match exists between the facilitator's image and style and that of the organization.

- The ideas the facilitator has to make your retreat effective.

It might be helpful to ask a board, committee or staff member that has experience facilitating retreats to sit in on the interviews. Such a person can help you assess the candidates' abilities to produce steak, and not just sizzle.

Yes, you want to ask enough questions to ensure that you are selecting the right facilitator, but you don't want to waste anyone's time – especially your own. If you have followed the recommended steps thus far, you have already narrowed the field to the cream of the crop. You don't need to spend two hours interviewing someone for a three-hour retreat. Plan your interviews for a timeframe that is commensurate with the length of the contract and the fees you expect to pay.

Unfortunately, there is no regulation of facilitators. Anyone can hang out a shingle. And, anyone marketing him or herself as a facilitator is probably a smooth talker. Do your homework. Ask for references and follow up on them.

Contracting with a Facilitator

Once you have decided to hire one of the facilitators do everyone a favor and get a written contract. It often seems unnecessary. After all, you've done your due diligence and you understand what has to be accomplished. Besides, you are only contracting for a short period of time – a couple of days at most. However, you will save yourself a lot of headaches if you have an agreement in writing. It doesn't have to be formal. It can be a simple letter outlining what each person or the organization commits to doing. The important thing is that you clarify expectations on both sides, including how the situation will be handled if they are not met.

The facilitator may have a standard contract or letter of agreement that he or she uses. If so, don't bother to reinvent the wheel as long as you are comfortable with it. While the contract or agreement may include many things, it should have at a minimum, the following:

- The desired outcomes.

- The date(s) of the retreat, as well as start and end times.

- The fee for services (this might be stated on a daily, hourly or project basis).

- A list of reimbursable expenses.

- A description of when the fees and expenses will be paid.

- The actions the facilitator commits to carry through for the organization.

- The commitments the organization makes to the facilitator to increase the chances of a successful retreat (e.g., calling the participants to remind them to attend).

- Cancellation policies.

- A list of any reports to be generated.

It is quite typical for facilitators to require a substantial percentage of the total fee – often half – at the point the contract is signed. Most expect to have the balance paid just before the retreat commences. Some facilitators refuse to "go on" if their check is not ready. Another "surprise" for some organization representatives is that many facilitators expect reimbursement of out-of-pocket expenses on top of their fees. You can avoid the shock if you negotiate the details. Negotiate an agreement that both parties feel is fair.

What You Should Expect From the Facilitator You Hire

You have already identified your key expectations in the contract. However, there are some basic professional behaviors that you can also expect. A facilitator should:

- Listen.
- Draw out the quiet individuals as well as move the conversation away from those who talk too much.
- Identify quickly when the conversation is moving off track and adroitly bring it back.
- Keep one eye on the clock so that the group is able to cover its agenda.
- Know when to inject some humor or a quick segue to keep a hot issue from boiling over into conflict.
- Confront problems directly and quickly, searching for win/win solutions.
- Have a range of conflict management styles upon which to draw if necessary.
- Incorporate a range of learning activities to meet all learning styles, if you are looking for someone to facilitate a training retreat.
- Be able to keep the retreat fun, interesting and purposeful.
- Treat everyone as equals.
- Avoid putting a participant down to show how clever or smart he or she is.
- Be where he or she promised to be when he or she promised to be there.

- Recommend appropriate resources.
- Admit if something is outside his or her area of expertise.
- Customize what he or she is doing for your organization.
- Reveal any conflicts of interest.
- Maintain confidentiality.
- Give you his or her best professional opinion, even if it is not what you want to hear.

Working with the Facilitator for Optimum Results

LAYING THE GROUNDWORK

Prepare the facilitator to do the best job he or she can do for you. Take the time to codify some of the answers to the questions that you asked yourself initially. You might use a briefing form to help organize your thoughts. While a sample form is included here, feel free to develop your own questions. (See *Facilitator Briefing Form*)

Give the answers to the facilitator along with the names of some other people to contact. It is always beneficial for the facilitator to talk with more than one person. It gives the facilitator a broader perspective. But, perhaps more important, it involves others and makes them more anxious to participate in the retreat knowing that they helped design the day. Give the facilitator the names of at least three people and aim for people with different viewpoints. A good mix is someone who has been around the organization for a long time and can give a historical view of what is needed, someone who is new who is not locked into "but this is how we've always done it," and a maverick. Contact those individuals ahead of time to let them know that the facilitator will be calling so that they can give some thought to the process rather than be forced to respond off the cuff.

Ask the facilitator what he or she needs logistically. Here, again, a form is helpful so that details don't fall through the cracks. *Facilitator Needs* is a sample of a logistics form. Determine ahead of time what the facilitator will bring and what you are expected to supply.

Facilitator Briefing Form

We appreciate your willingness to facilitate our retreat. We hope you find the following information helpful in preparing to work with our organization.

Organization: _____

Contact person: _____ Title: _____

Phone ( ): _____ Fax ( ): _____

Date(s) of the retreat: _____

Where the retreat will be held: _____

When the retreat begins: _____ ends: _____

Your portion of the meeting begins: _____ ends: _____

Dress for the retreat is: _____

Other than your own portion of the retreat, we would like to have you participate in the following activities: _____

You should plan on arriving at: _____ and expect to leave at: _____

The dress for these activities is: _____

Purpose of the retreat is: _____

Theme of the retreat is: _____

Topic immediately preceding your portion is: _____

Speaker: _____

Topic immediately following your portion: _____

Speaker: _____

Expected attendance (#): _____ Breakdown: Men _____ Women _____

Age range: _____ Different cultures represented: _____

Attendance is: _____ voluntary _____ suggested _____ mandated

Currently, the general level of knowledge and experience possessed by our participants on this subject is: _____

_____

You should know the following about those attending: _____

_____

Existing problems, competitive issues, or interesting dynamics of which you should be aware: _____

_____

Our objectives for your session are: _____

_____

We would like you to make the following 2 or 3 points in your session:

_____

_____

We would like you to plant the following "seeds" in your session:

_____

_____

We would like our participants to take the following action(s) as a result of your session: _____

_____

Our mission is: _____

_____

We are currently experiencing the following problems/breakthroughs/challenges:

_____

_____

We expect to make the following changes in our organization in the near future:

_____

_____

Please avoid mentioning the following issues, subjects, concepts or words:

_____

_____

You might want to incorporate some of the following in-house or market-specific language, jargon, acronyms or jokes to increase the sense of relevance to our participants: _____

_____

Other: _____

Facilitator Needs

We look forward to your involvement in our retreat on _____ .
(date)

We are expecting _____ participants. Your session will take place in the _____ Room, at the _____ .
(hotel/conference center)

So that we can arrange to have the room set up as you require it, please complete the following form and return it to our office by _____ .

If you require more than one room please complete a form for each room, and indicate the number of forms attached _____ . Thank you.

ROOM

____ Semi-circle		____ Board table
____ Horseshoe or "U" inside seating okay		____ Horseshoe or "U" no inside seating
____ Round tables set to capacity		____ Round tables set half full
____ Classroom		____ Chevron
____ Theater		____ Other: _____

EQUIPMENT

____ Flipchart stand # _____	____ Newsprint pad # _____
____ Overhead projector	____ Screen
____ Microphone: Type _____ # ____	
____ Podium (freestanding)	____ Podium (table top)
____ Slide projector	____ Tape recorder
____ Video player	____ TV monitor
____ Whiteboard	____ Electronic whiteboard
____ LCD projector	____ Laptop computer
____ Other: _____	

SUPPLIES

____ Markers (# ____)	____ Pencils/pens	____ Writing pads
____ Masking tape	____ Pins	

____ Handi-Tak (gum-like material that replaces tape or pins, available in office supply and drug stores)

____ Reports (Type _____)

____ Tent cards/name badges   Other: _____

DIVIDING RESPONSIBILITIES

Plan on working collaboratively with the facilitator. Do not expect to be able to turn over all responsibility for results to this person. But, on the other hand, don't hire a facilitator then expect to call all the shots. For optimum results, you will want to work together to define your outcomes and create a plan to reach them. This includes determining what changes are advisable, what steps are necessary to implement the changes, what timeline is recommended, and how best to minimize resistance to the changes. It also means working together to interpret the information that comes out of the retreat that you will use to accomplish everything stated above. While the facilitator can interpret the information from the perspective of both an unbiased observer and a technician, you know the players and the organization's history. You can ascribe nuances to responses that are critical to the final interpretation.

BEING HONEST ABOUT WHAT CAN REALISTICALLY BE ACCOMPLISHED

Be realistic about what the facilitator can accomplish. There are no magicians out there. People naturally resist change and results take time and commitment. Today most retreats are scheduled for three to six hours *with a meal.* This is not enough time to unfreeze old behaviors, teach new ones and refreeze these new, desired attitudes and actions. If you want to see change result from the retreat, ask the facilitator to build in accountability measures to encourage reinforcement of the desired behaviors. Consider your role in following through on the techniques he or she recommends. If possible, give the facilitator a role in implementation.

Keep the lines of communication open. If you are dissatisfied with the way things are going, raise the issue immediately when something can still be done about it. Good facilitators have thrown out their agendas on more than one occasion to better meet the needs of a group. They know they must be flexible. Ask to see if together you might come up with an alternate approach that would work for both of you. In the same way, if the facilitator approaches you with a problem, don't become defensive. Again, take a problem-solving approach to do what you can to optimize your retreat.

RESPECTING THE BUSINESS RELATIONSHIP

Start the relationship off right. While you may see it as your job to save your organization as much money as you can, expect to pay the facilitator's going rate – assuming, of course, that it is within the budget you determined before starting the interview process. Yes, some facilitators negotiate their fee and you should feel free to ask if they do. But, if you get a negative response to your question, let it go. Understand that working with organizations like yours is how facilitators earn the money to feed themselves and their families. They cannot give discounts to every client. Pushing them for a price cut will reflect poorly on your organization and create a sour taste that will last. Even if the facilitator accepts the contract, residual anger may affect the working relationship.

If you are happy with the work a facilitator does and you feel comfortable doing so, promote the person around your colleagues. Most facilitators find their work through referrals. They will appreciate your efforts on their behalf, and you will benefit from their appreciation. At the very least write a thank you letter to go in the facilitator's portfolio. Be as specific as possible about what he or she did for your organization that made a difference. Writing such a note is a simple task, yet it will leave the facilitator with a positive last impression of your organization. He or she will become your advocate in the community.

Conclusion

Retreats are here to stay. They will only grow in popularity. The right facilitator has the power to ensure that you use your time, talent and resources wisely. By understanding what a facilitator can do for you, recognizing when to go outside for help, having the confidence and skills to find the right facilitator, and knowing how to work with that person, you are opening your organization up to this power.

Bibliography

Block, Peter. (1981). *Flawless Consulting: A Guide to Getting Your Expertise Used.* San Diego, CA: Pfeiffer & Company.

Kibbe, Barbara and Setterberg, Fred. (1992). *Succeeding with Facilitators: Self Assessment for the Changing Nonprofit.* USA: The Foundation Center.

Moyers, Richard L. and Enright, Kathleen P. (1997). *A Snapshot of America's Nonprofit Boards: Results of the NCNB Nonprofit Governance Survey.* Washington DC: National Center for Nonprofit Boards.

Robinson, Dana Gaines and Robinson, James C. (1995). *Performance Consulting: Moving Beyond Training.* San Francisco, CA: Berrett-Koehler Publishers.

Temkin, Terrie (In Press). *A Charity Board's Guide to Using Consultants.* London: National Council of Voluntary Organizations.

Temkin, Terrie. (1997, May). Facilitator Stories with Happy Endings: Key Assessments to Make Before Contracting. *Strategic Governance,* 2(12), pp. 1-3.

Temkin, Terrie. (1999, November/December). In Search of the White Knight: Finding the Perfect Consultant. *Nonprofit World.*

Temkin, Terrie. (1998, February 2). Hiring a Facilitator? Have a Consultation. *Miami Herald Business Monday,* p. 8.

Temkin, Terrie. (1997, September). Roll Over Dogbert: Nonprofits Need the Old Facilitator. *Strategic Governance,* 3(4), pp. 1, 6-7.

Temkin, Terrie. (1998, February 16). There's a Facilitator Out There Who's Right for You. *Miami Herald Business Monday,* p. 10.

Terrie Temkin, Ph.D.

Terrie Temkin, Ph.D. brings 30 years of experience to her role as president of an international consulting firm, NonProfit Management Solutions, Inc. based in Hollywood, Florida since 1994. She has facilitated her share of retreats, working with approximately 40 - 60 organizations annually. As a perennial board member, she has also sat in on a number of board retreats that can only be described as a real cross-section of the good, the bad and the ugly.

Terrie is an accomplished public speaker and a dynamic group facilitator. She is an author with chapters in the two previous books in the *"Best of the Nonprofit Pros"* series, three booklets in press, and articles published in *Advancing Philanthropy, Board Member, E-Volunteerism, Nonprofit Board Report, Nonprofit World, and Strategic Governance,* to name just a few of the journals. Terrie is probably best known for her five-year stint as the "Ann Landers of the nonprofit world" when she wrote a biweekly newspaper column, "On Nonprofits," for the *Miami Herald.*

Terrie teaches governance in a masters-level nonprofit management program at Florida Atlantic University in Ft. Lauderdale, Florida. She is an approved facilitator for the Nonprofit Resource Institute of Palm Beach County (FL), has gone through the BoardSource (formerly National Center for Nonprofit Boards) facilitator's training program, and has taught consulting for Nova Southeastern University's School of Business and Entrepreneurship (Davie, FL).

Prior to starting NonProfit Management Solutions, Inc. Terrie served as executive director for Women's American ORT, Southeast District. The organization supports a worldwide network of technology schools. She also worked with the American Heart Association, the B'nai B'rith Youth Organization, and was a nationally-recognized trainer for Hospital Learning Centers.

Terrie Temkin, Ph.D.
NonProfit Management Solutions, Inc.
PO Box 7536, Hollywood, FL 33081
954-985-9489 • Toll-free: 866-985-9489 • Fax: 954-989-3442
E-mail: terriet@nonprofitmanagementsolutions.com
www.nonprofitmanagementsolutions.com

CHAPTER 3

Locating the Mine Fields and Digging for Gold: Pre-Retreat Interviews and Surveys

Thomas Bakewell, JD, CPA, MBA, MHA

Congratulations! You have been charged with the important responsibility of leading a successful retreat. Perhaps this is the biggest "contract" or engagement you have ever sold to a major new client, or maybe you are fulfilling an important charitable role by giving some of your leadership talent and time back to a community group or charity or maybe something in between. Whatever your situation, it's likely that your pre-retreat preparation will have a high probability of enhancing your chances of success in the retreat's outcome or results.

As you reflect on your work ahead in pre-retreat preparation for a successful event, thinking about what the end outcome or results could look like is always a great place to start.

Great questions most always provide the best answers, results, and outcomes. So as you start preparing for your retreat always take time for just a bit of quiet reflection on the work ahead at your favorite Starbuck's Coffee Shop or other peaceful spot – unless you are like my friend, Carol Weisman, and do your best reflective thinking with a cell phone glued to your ear, a car or plane seat strapped to your body, and an "audience" just around the corner. As she would say, "Works for me" . . . and it does work for her!

Let's consider some of the key questions you would want to ask yourself and perhaps others as you prepare for this retreat:

KEY QUESTIONS TO CONSIDER

- Who is my client?

- Who is my audience?

- What would success look like for this retreat?

- What do I need to find out to get the job done? Better yet, what information would help me do a great job with this retreat?

- What do I hope to accomplish?

- What was I contracted or engaged to do?

- All things considered, what would best serve the client organization you are working with?

- What would a good survey instrument look like for this engagement?

- How do I locate the mine fields and dig for the gold?

- What do I do with the information?

Who is my client?

Don't laugh. This is a serious question, especially if you have an ongoing consulting relationship beyond the retreat. And the answer to this question is usually complex. Is it the Board of Trustees? Is it the staff? The CEO? The person engaging your services? The person paying for your services? All of the above?

Think seriously about who your client is. And if you are confused about who your client is in a complex relationship reach out to a professional peer for input and dialog.

Who is my audience?

At the simplest level, this question can be answered with very straightforward information. Who will be in the room for the retreat? But even the most basic audience information can help clarify your work at hand.

At a minimum, consider doing a basic retreat profile including:

- Size of group;

- Trustees/directors vs. staff;

- Spouses in audience;

- Male/female ratio of audience;

- Responsibilities, roles and titles in audience;

- Names and titles of key "players";

- Expected dress for audience participants;

- Special needs, i.e. sign language;

- And so forth.

What would a success look like for this retreat?

Think about the real reasons this retreat is occurring, what the organization is objectively asking for and why you were hired. Is this a special moment in the life of the organization, such as their first formal board retreat ever or is it the 75th annual alumnae association volunteer meeting for your alma mater? Or are the feds about to close them down? In other words, is it business as usual simply requiring routine facilitation or far more than that? Is there trouble in Dodge City waiting to emerge, a seriously demoralized organization and staff or worse? Or is this a healthy and thriving organization eager to do their work?

If you can gain insights into the group and organization you will be leading at the retreat and get a solid feel for where they are in their life cycle, history, and operations before entering the room, you can get a better idea of what success might look like to them with this retreat.

Will success with this retreat require a carefully planned expert process to draw information and dialog out or do you simply need to show up and count on the participants to do the hard work and engage in lively conversation.

Will success mean a clear process completed on time with no surprises, hiccups or hot topics? Or will success mean addressing some of the organization's toughest dilemmas or unspoken issues and myths?

A key tip to determining what success would look like for the retreat is to simply ask the key players the following question. "If this retreat were a huge success, what would be accomplished and what would that look like?"

As you clarify your picture of what a success would look like for this retreat, don't forget to include the process for getting objective feedback at the end of the retreat. Thinking about and preparing your closing survey instrument while determining what success would look like for this retreat can generate good ideas and bear much fruit up front. Starting with the end in mind can help focus your work on the overall process and provide good insights and results.

At Exhibit 1 (see the end of this chapter), you will find one of the simple closing survey forms I've used over the years. As you review this form ask yourself what information you would add to have a good closing survey form for your work.

What do I need to find out to get the job done? Better yet, what information would help me do a great job with this retreat?

Now that you have contemplated and perhaps gained clarity on who your client is; who your audience is; and what success would look like for this retreat, you should have a good picture emerging as to what information and data you will need to have and find for the job you want to accomplish.

Is your client a strong thriving organization with healthy operations at all levels of its system? Or is it an organization that's been going sideways for a decade and needs some real work in a number of key areas; or is your client organization just getting by, in operating distress, and suffering from outright denial of it problems?

A simple gathering of basic knowledge of your client's system in the key areas of strategy, operations and finances will offer valuable guidance for preparing preretreat interviews and surveys that will help you locate the mine fields and dig for gold.

As you do your work gathering the preretreat information, always contemplate what "level of system" you are dealing with for your work and retreat. Are you truly dealing with the entire organization and all of its constituencies from top to bottom and all of their combinations and permutations, including the board, management, employees, staff, advisors, volunteers, customers (whether clients, patients, students, etc.) or are you focused on some select group or level of the client's systems, such as only the board of directors or only the management team.

Always contemplate what level of system for the entire organization your work is intended to encompass and touch upon. Levels of system include individuals, dyads, triads, small groups, large groups, departments, divisions, job title, job levels, subsidiaries, corporate entities, employees, executives, directors, trustees, customers, clients, advisors, stakeholders, shareholders, volunteers, members of the community and on and on.

For information regarding strategy, operations and finances, it is not necessary to be a sophisticated MBA or financial analyst to gain a simple knowledge and basic information in these areas.

Straight forward general questions regarding the strengths and weaknesses of the organization often times can prompt good information and insights into the organization's operations and finances. A similar simple question that provokes good information is to simply ask what's working and what's not.

Beyond simple questions more specific questions can be developed to focus on a particular area. For example, several key questions regarding strategy could include:

- Does your current strategy fit competitive realities?;

- Has your performance been less than potential?;

- Are there key dilemmas that need to be worked out in the organization?;

- Is the organization focused internally instead of on customers and competitors?;

- Is your overall strategy or operating model thriving or failing?

A simple survey instrument is found at Exhibit 2. This Exhibit outlines a simple way that a person with rudimentary skills in the areas of finance, operations, or fundraising could get a good grasp on the organization's position as a whole from a very basic viewpoint. Simple survey instruments can be prepared for any number of other types of questions or survey. For example, very simple but similar survey instruments could be developed in areas such as assessing potential for fundraising or simple focus groups regarding various information on the organization.

What do I hope to accomplish?

Once again as you contemplate your retreat, you should think deeply about what you hope to accomplish. Does your skill set, knowledge and initial research tell you that there is a major piece of work lurking here that is just crying for your attention? Or is this a very focused, specific, and limited task that you have been assigned regarding the retreat. Bring this issue of what you hope to accomplish into clear focus before moving on.

What was I contracted or engaged to do?

Asking yourself what was I contracted or engaged to do is self protective behavior of the highest order and important for a reality check before you engage in your work with a client. This issue deals with the dilemma of giving the client what they want versus what they need. You as a top consultant preparing to lead a retreat may be well aware that your client organization has substantial issues and needs much beyond what you would hope to accomplish. That's wonderful. But ask yourself once again. What was I contracted or engaged to do? No matter how talented you are, you can't put 10 lbs. in a five lb. bag and you can't achieve peace in the middle east in an afternoon!

If you have been contracted or engaged to do a very limited piece of work then you're headed for trouble in one way or the other by digging into work beyond the scope of your engagement. Trouble could present itself in a number of ways. It might be as complex as surfacing issues that the client doesn't want to deal with or trouble could be as simple as you pursuing a major piece of work for which the client is grateful but unwilling to pay.

A good test to apply to yourself to stay on track is to make sure that you have the basics that you are going to undertake in a written engagement letter or contract. You will find more information about engagement letters and contracting in Chapter Two of this book by Dr. Terrie Temkin.

All things considered, what would best serve the client organization?

Answering this question about what would best serve the client organization is a final check to make sure your ego is in place and the client is being well served. Please know that by referencing the need for one to check his/her ego at several places throughout the process does not mean you are out of line with desiring to do a substantial piece of work. Just remember, the work is always about the client and not you. Conversely, by asking yourself what would best serve the client organization you may find yourself faced with situations that could give you pause from an integrity point of view or work plan point of view. For example, are you being asked to undertake a piece of work that you know is simply not possible to be accomplished within the time or financial budget assigned? Are you being asked to undertake a piece of work that for various reasons might not be respectful of the client organization and people involved if the matter is handled in the process that the organization is requesting or proposing? This is the point where you sort through the chaff and become comfortable with the overall process and engagement you're signing up for. And if you have serious reservations, don't hesitate to reach to a professional peer for good impartial input.

What would a good survey instrument look like for this engagement?

Exhibits 2 and 3 attached represent simple survey instruments.

Exhibit 4 represents a more comprehensive survey instrument. By reviewing these three exhibits together, you can get an idea of a wide range of survey instruments and can prepare a document properly scoped to your engagement.

In reviewing the comprehensive survey instrument at Exhibit 4, you can see how using this instrument to interview eight to 10 people from a client organization with interviews of some 30 to 60 minutes each could produce an enormous amount of valuable information.

How do I locate the mine fields and dig for the gold?

Once you've decided what good solid interview or survey instruments might look like and the scope of information you would like to obtain, there are lots of ways to undertake the actual process of doing the work. For example, interviews can be held in person, by phone, individually or in group sessions. Surveys can be handled by mail, e-mail, or fax. A key element to keep in mind when undertaking the work is that if questions are framed properly and clients genuinely believe they're dealing in confidence with a person of integrity, you should expect a great deal of information, much candor, and a good dose of reality. Often interviews and surveys can produce information for the client organization that has not surfaced in a formal fashion before.

And what might those mine fields look like or those nuggets of gold look like? A few sample nuggets of gold and mine fields from past experiences include:

Nuggets of Gold	Mine Fields
• Super talent at all levels of the organization	• A "secret" financial problem or crisis that is just around the corner that no one is talking about
• An organization where the people really care about each other at all levels of the system	• A top executive who has retired on the job
• An organization that is thriving	• An organization that is failing and doesn't know what to do about it
• An organization where people are looking to give money and added support	• A "tradition bound" organization not reacting to important changes in its market place
• An organization that is thriving mightily, but has one simple matter that needs to be tended to	• Executives fighting, pointing fingers, and not working as a team
• Etc., Etc., Etc.	• Etc., Etc., Etc.

Another critical factor in having a success is to ask yourself who you should interview. Do you interview all current leaders, potential leaders, and possible "problem" leaders. Determining who you interview is critical to results and success.

What do I do with the information?

This is where you earn your pay. How you respectfully handle the critical information you have learned about an organization and feed it back to them will have a huge impact on the success or failure of any retreat and consulting engagement.

A key component of any successful retreat and consulting engagement is having a "sponsor" within the organization who can work closely with and coach you on challenges in undertaking a successful engagement.

As they used to say in the introduction to *Mission Impossible* "Good Luck, Mr. Phelps should you elect to undertake this assignment."

EXHIBIT 1

TO: GROUP RETREAT TEAM

FROM: CONSULTANT

RE: CONSULTANT RETREAT REVIEW FOLLOW UP
SURVEY

Consultant was engaged to help in our planning and retreat efforts.

Please evaluate consultant's work by completing this short survey.

1. On a scale of "1 to 5" with "1 being poor," and "5 being
excellent," how would you rate consultant on the following:

Level of Competence	1 . . . 2 . . . 3 . . . 4 . . . 5 . . .
Level of Ethical Standards	1 . . . 2 . . . 3 . . . 4 . . . 5 . . .
"Results Achieved"	1 . . . 2 . . . 3 . . . 4 . . . 5 . . .
"Process Used"	1 . . . 2 . . . 3 . . . 4 . . . 5 . . .
Overall satisfaction	1 . . . 2 . . . 3 . . . 4 . . . 5 . . .
Understanding of our business	1 . . . 2 . . . 3 . . . 4 . . . 5 . . .
Accessibility and responsiveness to your needs	1 . . . 2 . . . 3 . . . 4 . . . 5 . . .
Quality service on timely basis	1 . . . 2 . . . 3 . . . 4 . . . 5 . . .
Adherence to agreed upon plans	1 . . . 2 . . . 3 . . . 4 . . . 5 . . .
Flexibility to meet our changing needs	1 . . . 2 . . . 3 . . . 4 . . . 5 . . .
Business advice	1 . . . 2 . . . 3 . . . 4 . . . 5 . . .
Politically astute	1 . . . 2 . . . 3 . . . 4 . . . 5 . . .
Level of knowledge and experience	1 . . . 2 . . . 3 . . . 4 . . . 5 . . .
Courteousness and helpfulness	1 . . . 2 . . . 3 . . . 4 . . . 5 . . .
Showed up on time	1 . . . 2 . . . 3 . . . 4 . . . 5 . . .
Did what was promised	1 . . . 2 . . . 3 . . . 4 . . . 5 . . .
Finished what was started	1 . . . 2 . . . 3 . . . 4 . . . 5 . . .
Said please and thank you	1 . . . 2 . . . 3 . . . 4 . . . 5 . . .

2.   What were consultant's strengths?

3.   What were consultant's weaknesses?

4.   What could consultant have done to improve this engagement?

5.   What could our management have done to improve this engagement?

6.   Suggestions for consultant's improvement:

7.   Would you recommend consultant to your professional peers and business associates?

_____ Yes   _____ No

If yes, why and to whom?

If no, why not?

EXHIBIT 2

SIMPLE SURVEY INSTRUMENT
HOW DO YOU RATE OUR POSITION?

Failing		*Maintaining*		*Thriving*
1	2	3	4	5

ORGANIZATIONALLY

• As of two years ago?   • As of today?

Score   Score

Comments: _____

OPERATIONALLY

• As of two years ago?   • As of today?

Score   Score

Comments: _____

FINANCIALLY

• As of two years ago?   • As of today?

Score   Score

Comments: _____

HOW DO YOU RATE OUR POSITION?

Failing		*Maintaining*		*Thriving*
1	2	3	4	5

QUALITY SERVICE

• As of two years ago?   • As of today?

Score   Score

Comments: _____

STAFFING

• As of two years ago?   • As of today?

Score   Score

Comments: _____

SPIRITUALLY

• As of two years ago?   • As of today?

Score   Score

Comments: _____

OVERALL

• As of two years ago?   • As of today?

Score   Score

Comments: _____

EXHIBIT 3

Board or Management Team or Department Head or etc.

SIMPLE SURVEY INSTRUMENT
HOW DO YOU RATE OUR POSITION?
OUTCOMES

	1 Failing	2	3 Maintaining	4	5 Thriving
Organizationally			2.8	3.9	
Operationally			2.8	3.5	
Financially			3.2	3.8	
Quality Service		2.2	3.1		
Staffing			3.0	3.3	
Spiritually			2.8	3.8	
Overall			2.8	3.7	

Note: Nonbold numbers two years ago; numbers in **bold** are current score

EXHIBIT 4

Board or Management Team or Department Heads or etc.

COMPREHENSIVE SURVEY INSTRUMENT
Interview Outline – Board of Directors

1. Do you perceive the need for significant change in your organization at this time?

    - How urgent is this need?

    - How aware are other stakeholders of the need for change in your organization?
      Other board members?
      Management team?
      Middle management/directors?
      Line staff?
      Volunteers?
      Funders?

    - Would major change be supported by
      Board of Directors?
      Management Team?
      Middle management/directors?

2. How do you rate the overall operating efficiency of your organization? 1.0 failing/5.0 thriving

3. Can you give me a snapshot of your perspective on the finances of your organization?

    - Where are they?

    - Where should they be?

    - Holding, gaining, sliding?

- Thoughts on cash reserves
- Thoughts on debt
- Thoughts on staffing
- Thoughts on capital expenditures

4. What are your organization's top three strengths?

   a.

   b.

   c.

5. What are your organization's top three weaknesses?

   a.

   b.

   c.

6. Where has your organization been unexpectedly successful?

7. Can you identify any significant innovations that have occurred at your organization over the past few years?

8. Does your organization have a good feel for its primary customer base?

   - Has this primary customer base changed?

   - Has your organization appropriately responded to this change in customer base?

9. Is your organization meetings its goals?

10. Where do you see your organization?

    1.0   Failing

    3.0   Status Quo/Maintenance

    5.0   Thriving

11. Tell me your thoughts on your organization and its information system needs.

12. Tell me your thoughts on your organization and its retail sales and recent implementation.

13. Where would you like to see your organization in three years?

14. Is your organization utilizing your talents?

Thomas Bakewell, JD, CPA, MBA, MHA

Tom Bakewell looks like an ordinary guy. He is not. His idea of a good time is somewhat unusual. A devout Christian, when heading to the beach for vacation, his choice of reading tends to be religious philosophy. When heading to work, his favorite thing to do is massive turnarounds. He does the institutional equivalent of parallel parking the Q.E.II.

Tom has the skills and the background to work with organizations which need a 360 look at their structure and competencies. Tom's credentials include a JD, CPA, MBA and MHA. In addition to his other nonprofit clients, Tom has been instrumental in working in depth with over 30 colleges and universities to re-think their financial strategies to be better prepared for tomorrow's students.

Tom worked for years with the Daughters of Charity in top legal and financial positions during the formation of the nation's largest health care system.

Tom has served on the board of a public television station, a university, a hospital, a long term health care system and several privately held companies.

Tom manages to keep his figure despite living with his beautiful wife Julia, a professional cook. After spending his days strategizing with nonprofits, eating amazing dinners prepared by Julia, he spends the rest of his time playing with his four-year-old son Myles, his six-year-old Catherine and Chester the dog.

Tom Bakewell
7777 Bonhomme, Suite 1710
Clayton, MO 63105
Phone: 314-725-5552
E-mail: ThomasBakewell@hotmail.com

CHAPTER 4

Foods that Build Community

M. Rose Jonas, Ph.D.
and
Ellen Sweets

Introduction

Between us we have more years than we care to tell you fussing with food. We have led board retreats and training seminars (Rose), and written about food (Ellen, with the *Dallas Morning News* and the Neiman Marcus chefscatalog.com). Together we've co-authored *Fast Friends, Fragrant Kitchens*, and both of us have lifted a convivial glass or two in celebration of some pretty outrageous food events.

In planning your retreat you are responsible for a wall-to-wall experience, and that includes the food your folks eat. It can account for a satisfied or snarly group waving good-by at the retreat's end. So be as careful with the type and timing of vittles as you are with each day's timetable and icebreaker exercises.

No matter what you decide to do about food, the focus must always be on the group and its experience. Rose chaired an event for a community organization that was open to the public and generally attracted several hundred people. As we stewed over the menu, one of the committee members said, "Look, a year from now, they're not going to remember the food. They'll remember the speaker and whether they had fun with their friends."

Attendees at your retreat might not recall whether you served sea bass or lavosh sandwiches, but they'll remember if the food was inadequate or boring. You can achieve enormous creativity, energy, instructive fun, fond memories and serious points with the food you serve. If you're not careful and thoughtful, you can also wind up with cranky participants. Take good care of them so they can perform at their best.

The Role of Food at a Board Retreat

You don't especially want food to be a central feature of your retreat. You don't want them dawdling *á la* the French Riviera over espresso, brie and fruit, but you don't want them to feel as if they've been hustled through a New York City falafel stand either. If an army moves on its stomach, a well-fed conference responds to good food. You want them to be nourished, refreshed, relaxed, and able to say on task. You want food to be background, but a comforting presence.

Anyone who grew up in the South knows the cultural rule that the dining room curtains must match the napkins must match the Jell-O salad. In the same way your food should match what your retreat is trying to accomplish. Think about the organization's mission and the goal for the retreat. If the group has worked under severe pressure, should the food have a fun theme? If the board doesn't get along, should everyone have a stint in the kitchen as part of an exercise in cooperation? If the group is concerned about poverty law, should they eat the kinds of meals the organization's clients have every day? Should they barter beads for beans? If you have a high-powered board, will they want *petits four* and brandy? It depends on the participants and what you want from them.

Food gives you an opportunity for play, drama, and unforgettable moments. Clerical staff at a frantically paced medical clinic loved their Halloween-Day teambuilding at which we created a kids' haunted house. Blindfolded, they plunged hands into bowls of "eyeballs" (peeled grapes), "brains" (cold spaghetti) and candy worms. They bobbed for doughnut holes on a string. They took home a goody bag. They still talk about it.

Get Them Going. . .and Keep Them Going

Food should be part of your retreat scene pretty much from the moment participants arrive. You could do what some wedding parties do, have a hospitality bag in the room if the group will have a several-day stay. Include the agenda, information about the area, ground rules (which they review at the first session), how they can reach each other. Give them bottled water, raisins, a candy bar, some crackers, a piece of fruit, maybe some local information from the Chamber of Commerce, or a snack food that's loved in the region. (Ever had a Moon Pie?)

Keep tea, water, coffee and snacks available throughout the day. Keep fruit, mints, leftover "Trick or Treat" candy and pretzels on a table in the back of the room as pick-me-ups for the 3 o'clock tumble from attentiveness. Don't over-feed them, but don't look at food as a way to shave a few dollars from the budget. You may not want to pop for breakfast, but if you don't you'll make the morning a yawning chasm between the opening hello and the lunch bell. Spend a few dollars on crackers or bagels. It's a small price to pay for their attention; their grumbling stomachs won't drown out the facilitator's voice.

If it's a one-day meeting and there's no afternoon snack, tell them if they work hard and get all of the conference work done, they can go home an hour early. No group has EVER failed to make that deadline. They DO get the work done and they DON'T go sniffing for cakes and cookies.

What Food Should You Serve?

Pay attention to locale and the season. Facilitators all have horror stories like this: A day of strategic planning, held at a dark and stuffy city club in the midst of a brutally hot July. Lunch was in the musty dining room: pork chops, stuffing, apples, macaroni salad, carrot medallions and chocolate cream pie. A meal guaranteed to require a nap. None of the participants cared about the flip charts after 3:00. We had to end the day early. We reconvened at the client's conference room next morning, and – buzzed on coffee – whizzed through an afternoon's work in less than two hours.

So, think LIGHT in the summer, fragrant and substantial but not too heavy in the cooler months. If you're in the mountains, remember that altitude affects people and their digestive and respiratory systems: no heavy foods midday for sure. Bear in mind that when people have traveled a distance, they love someone making the extra effort to provide signature foods from the region. Tennessee pulled pork sandwiches with Cole slaw; clam chowder in Boston, Ted Drewes ice cream in St. Louis; Queen Anne cherries in Seattle. Any conference in Texas has to include a barbecue.

Don't Shut Them Down

Think twice about filling them full of sugar – cinnamon rolls in the morning, pie for lunch, cookies in the afternoon. Food like that used to be the hallmark of the long off-site, especially in areas proud of their home cookin'. Facilitators would compare rueful notes about attention lost and pounds gained. These days, participants might even bypass the Danish in deference to blueberry or bran muffins.

Hearty eaters love lots of food and will storm through the noshes with great swigs of black coffee – the real stuff – but by 10 in the morning, they develop that trouble-on-the-playground glint in their eyes. Before you know it, you're dodging paper clips and spit wads. You definitely lose their attention. We give you more detail later, but menu suggestions would be bagels, baby Danish, muffins and fruit for breakfast. At lunch give them light dessert choices, not "death-by-chocolate" cake. And fruit and cookies in the afternoon. Keep them hydrated with water, and revved up with soda (or pop, depending on where you live) and coffee.

What About a Working Lunch?

Don't have a working lunch or lunch in the room where you're working. Groups want to get the most from their session and their time together, so they may ask to work through. Don't let them. They will seldom fare well munching a ham sandwich over budget variance reports. Their minds and hearts become engaged with the work at hand. Their bodies need a break. Without it, they'll be like naughty kids. They'll decide to leave early; they'll nap with one eye open while hearing departmental PowerPoint presentations; they'll quarrel with every suggestion.

On rare occasions you can have a working lunch. If they've been out all morning (and we mean <u>out</u>. . .in the woods, in the town, conducting individual research for bringing back to the group. . .in other words, away from each other), then a working lunch could be just the ticket. They'll want to share their stories and what they've learned; they will happily chat over casual sandwiches. It will be a welcome contrast to their morning, and a "together" setting will harness and focus that energy.

Another "food-in-the-room" situation is if you're doing an Open Space Technology experience. Open Space works well with large groups (100+!). Its design allows participants to range through a facility working on issues according to their interests. Lunch isn't a formal affair. A cold buffet is set out late morning, and people are expected to stop and nosh when they feel like it, alone or with others.

How long should the meal break be? The group's leader will often want to whittle it to 30 minutes. Can't be done. They have to wash their hands, get their food, schmooze over lunch, call their office, suck a breath mint, find the fresh air they need, maybe check out of the hotel. If it's a single day experience, 45 minutes to eat a good box lunch is reasonable. If it's a week-long experience, give them an hour and a half. They'll think it's too long, then they'll never come back on time.

Should they be on their own for lunch? Generally not, unless you know the Speedy Eats around the corner really is. It's too hard to herd them, especially if the event lasts a few hours. Keep 'em in the corral.

Who Chooses the Food?

You will find lots of accumulated wisdom at the first Retreat Planning Committee meeting. Have members come prepared with names of facilities and costs, good catering services, menu suggestions, contact names and phone numbers. Develop a budget. If there's time and the event warrants it, have catering companies present menu options. Schedule a food tasting.

For a one-day session, you'll need breakfast, mid-morning and afternoon snacks, lunch. For overnights, include an opening dinner, the hospitality bags, any late-night snacks.

Divide up the responsibilities. Who will plan and fetch and who will help on site (including the inevitable clean-up)? Discuss creative ways to save money. Will a local business provide one or more of the meals, or pony up for the drinks? Does a local store support your cause enough that it will donate bags or product samples? If a vendor wants to make a sales pitch about software, you may get your afternoon snack covered. Never forget the participants or the goals for the meeting, though. Those come first.

What should you do if you're a committee of one, if the retreat will be held in a distant or unfamiliar locale? Never do this alone. Planning takes longer and you get fewer ideas if you're talking to yourself. Everybody knows somebody. You have a friend who's great at doing this; take her to lunch and pump her for ideas. By the time they clear away the iced tea, you'll have a plan. Or, you have a colleague in the meeting's location. Make a call. Get the information, or get passed on to someone who knows. The sales and catering staffs of hotels are generally eager, helpful, friendly. There's lots of informal help around. Reach for it.

You might not be the right person for making and bird-dogging all the plans. Perhaps the organization has an administrative assistant who can lend a hand, if not do the bulk of the work.

Keep track of progress during the planning stages. You've taken on the job, and the responsibility is yours till the end, so you need to know what's going to happen when and by whom. When you arrive at the retreat, get the planning sheet from the sales and catering manager or whoever is overseeing the event so you can make any last-minute changes. Stay aware of how closely the session is following the plan so you can take care of any problems that crop up.

Who Brings the Food,
You, the Center or the Pizza Guy?

You generally want the participants to bring only a good attitude, not the food. Food-toting can become an organizational nightmare, and imagine a high-powered executive board member happily volunteering to bring the mac 'n' cheese. Most of the time, folks expect to walk in, empty their brains, get served, tussle with issues and leave.

There are times when the participants might pack a cooler and burp the Tupperware: The organization has a miniscule budget. The meeting is at a rustic cabin. The point of the meeting is to structure more personal relationships. If this is the case, decide who sets up, dishes out, and cleans up. Make sure the work and the cash outlays are evenly distributed, and the teaching points about "team cooperation" get made. If the topic is "multicultural us" let the Scots bring scones, the Greeks rice pilaf, the Indians *balti beef kofta*, and let everyone explain their food. Discuss what brings people together, and how challenging that is, with something as simple as food.

This collegial hash-slinging can feel more like a campout than participants may want, however, in which case, find the local pizza guy. Unless you're retreating on a bumpy-road ranch, there's a 555-FOOD service that delivers from local restaurants. Make the plans ahead of time, avoid letting the participants make food choices (you'll go mad counting turkey vs. tuna sandwiches, and of COURSE the board president's order won't show up). Check on it several hours ahead of when you need it, but keep your own focus on the meeting. Your deep insights and thoughtful work are needed there.

Managing the 3 O'clock Slump

It's 3 o'clock in the afternoon. You hope the facilitator has kept people up doing things since lunch, talking rather than listening, creating rather than passively absorbing. A post-lunch video is just a cover for naptime. Whatever has happened since lunch, the people who have been scrunched into an airless room have become wobbly-headed and crabby; they're dozing, doodling, moo-ing out the window. They need their milk and cookies or they want to go home.

Give them their snack. If you can make it relevant to the material, that's great. At a seminar for an association of state agencies human resource directors, one of the points was that, since they could not compete with the higher salaried market out there, they had to emphasize the personal touch. The theme of the discussion was "Make them cookies," and that's what they got. Homemade chocolate chip cookies, to show how good a personal gesture feels. Each table had its own bag, and the group got cookies, a break, and the point.

Doubletree Hotels make chocolate chip cookies as a signature, for guests and for meeting participants. Retreat houses often like offering such sweets. It's a nice touch. You might want to bring nibbles like mints, mini-chocolate bars, pretzels to stave off that mid-afternoon, low-blood-sugar dip.

Regarding the Veggie-only, Chicken-only, Vegan, Allergic, Caf and Decaf Participants

You will facilitate retreats in different parts of the country. In the solid, sensible Midwest, it might be fine if you just rip open the Wonder Bread, cut the horns off the steer and run in the steak. Don't, however, try this in the west where you will be nagged to death about food, drink, location, amenities and air quality. You must anticipate and plan for widely varying food preferences. The contingent that flew in from Chicago just will NOT care for the cheese grits casserole that's much beloved in Memphis. The union guys are just NOT going to eat another rubber chicken.

Giving the problem its less flip due, someone who has a severe seafood sensitivity could become seriously ill if a shrimp finds its way into the risotto. Lactose intolerance among many adults makes chicken á la king a bad menu choice. Vegans and vegetarians and those who keep kosher make those food decisions for reasons important to them.

What to do? In the invitation, ask participants to let staff know of any food requirements or sensitivities. Talk with the kitchen folks to ensure they don't slip a shrimp into the bisque. If you need kosher food, the local kosher butcher can tell you where to find a box lunch. If you have vegetarians or allergic people, they're accustomed to exercising a vigilant self-responsibility, but it's a nice touch to call and find out food needs.

Getting What You Want from the Food Service People

You might be flying in the day before an overnight off-site. Maybe you aren't familiar with the retreat center. . If you can talk ahead of time by phone with the food and beverage manager, that's great. At the event a cheery hello to the morning crew is the minimum and a must. The people who do this for a living usually love it. They like the chance to be creative and show their stuff. They like the appreciation they too seldom receive. So, YOU be the one who reaches out, talks about the event and its requirements, and follows up. At the end of the day bring someone from the facility into the dining room and give them applause. Food preparers work too hard but remain too anonymous; let them know you appreciate them having done their best for you.

The Facilitator's Food

Ask the facilitator, "Do you want to eat with us?" They often don't, and it's nothing personal. They've been in the spotlight for the last several hours. It might be nice to get a breather; also, there's often next-segment planning to do and the meal break is good for that. Also, the participants can become shy and careful of their behavior – as if the minister got stuck at their wedding reception table.

Some facilitators may want to dine with you, especially at dinner when there's more down time. They know everyone, they want the company, they're prepared for the section to come. Other facilitators may be particular about food and bring their own: bottled water, cans of tuna, fruit. They're on stage so they feed themselves only what won't turn on them later in the day. So the bean nacho appetizer everyone's noshing could send the facilitator gasping from the room later.

Menus

Let's recap: When you consider food for retreats, you have to think, not only about food sensitivities, but also about variety, convenience, fast service, pick-up-ability, the snooze factor and digestibility. Here are some menu suggestions:

Breakfast

Juice (Tomato, grapefruit, orange, cranberry, apple). They'll snarf up the orange and apple. They'll mix the cranberry and apple – and the cranberry and orange.

Bagels with cream cheese. Always popular. Include "lite" cream cheese.

Small Danish or muffins, or coffee cake cut in small portions. Head off the carbo-snoozing.

A fresh-fruit bowl or cut-up fruit

Coffee (caf and decaf), tea (pekoe _and_ herbal) with lemon, cream, sugar and sweetener (pink stuff AND blue stuff).

What about a hearty breakfast instead of a cold buffet? Honey, you just haven't LIVED until you've squeezed a crowd of energetic people into a too-small room for an entire day that began with a hot breakfast. You'll watch bilious fatigue come over them as the sausage, scrambled eggs, hash browns and sticky buns slosh around their coffee-acid stomachs. Try to get them to care; go ahead. I dare you. Your desire to show them how special they are will result in something akin to coma.

Ongoing

Coffee (make sure it's kept fresh) and tea

Bottled water

Soft drinks (regular and diet). You might as well have it available from the beginning. For some people, this _is_ their morning coffee.

Lunch

Menu? Buffet? Pizza? Happy Meals? On their own? It depends on the agenda, where you are and what you need for "flow." If they've been together for an intense morning, they might value a quick cold cut, build-your-own sandwich so they can go for a walk before the 1 o'clock lock-up proceeds. If, as is often the case with boards, they don't know one another, then make the meal a time for that. Consider the reality of group dining, however. The person to your left and right and perhaps just across from you can chortle at your *bon mots*; but you never get to meet the chap at the end of the table, here from the Badlands. Set place cards. Put dessert and coffee somewhere else so they'll find new friends for conversation. Give them a lunchtime assignment to discuss with three others.

Don't let them order from the menu. If the wait staff is slow, the afternoon schedule could get squeezed. Plan set choices – a meat, a vegetable and a fish or chicken option – so the kitchen will be prepared in advance. Or do a buffet, so they can choose for themselves:

Salad and dressings and relishes

Several cheese choices and cold meats (roast beef, turkey, ham)

Vegetarian pasta

Hot vegetable

Rolls and bread

Bite-size desserts (cookies, brownies, lemon squares)

Whole fruit (re-serve leftovers at the break)

P.M. Break

Throughout the day you've kept the coffee and tea going. By this time people have generally had enough. Give them a fresh or new sweet, soft drinks, water and fruit again. You'll be surprised how fast the water and fruit disappear.

Dinner

Dinner is usually an expensive proposition when you have a multi-day affair. If participants are local, let them go home. If you have evening sessions, make overnight stays optional. If you meet after dinner, allow two to two-and-a-half hours for dinner, planning to keep them till 9:30 (your facilitator is a slave driver). In this case have the meal served on the premises. Keep the menu simple and not over-sauced. Offer something for vegetarians, a beef and chicken entree, a carbohydrate and a salad. Have dessert and coffee in a lounge near the meeting rooms. We're not anti-drinking, but alcohol is often not your friend at a retreat. A glass of wine or sherry between the afternoon session and dinner is fine; so is wine with the meal; so is a post-evening-session liqueur. But make alcohol available with a VERY light hand. The stories we could tell you about boozy hasty words and broken relationships. . .!

If yours is a weeklong retreat, the evening meals will have a definite flavor. Dinner Sunday will be light and happy, with mingling and maybe icebreakers. Monday night the group will still be curious, though it's usually a tough day and they won't be in love with the facilitator or each other. By Tuesday they will have made new friends, and be having a good time. Wednesday is "hump day," they're halfway to home. They get tired and unruly, so they must have Wednesday afternoon and evening off, with dinner on their own. If they are in a locale they're not likely to visit again, it gives them at least a few hours to explore. Thursday evening should be a box lunch picnic by the river, weather permitting, or something casual off-premises or grilled hot dogs followed by a talent show because they're ready to burst. Friday, don't count on many of them for the concluding lunch. They would flap their arms if they thought it would make the journey home faster.

Should you have a hospitality suite? Probably not, because of the expense, unless there isn't a lobby or other area where participants can congregate. They need outside-the-meeting talking opportunities. If you do have a hospitality suite, you can often bring in your own drinks and snacks. Get a couple of volunteers (strong ones) to haul in the coolers, coffee makers, ice, drinks, paper plates and napkins, glasses, cookies, chips, nuts, string cheese and fruit. Get two more volunteers to staff the suite and bus it when party detritus begins to overwhelm. Be sure to have hauler-out volunteers, too.

Okay, since our cooking memoir, *Fast Friends, Fragrant Kitchens*, has recipes, we can't resist giving you a couple of recipes for hospitality suite goodies. They'll look familiar; they seem to show up in all church cook books, but they're fast; they're portable, they're delicious:

Texas Buttermilk Sheet Cake

Spray a jelly roll pan (10 x 15, disposable!) with cooking spray. Heat oven to 350°. Put into a large measuring cup and microwave till butter melts:
    2 sticks butter
    3 T cocoa

In a mixing bowl combine:
    2 c. sugar
    2 c. sifted flour
    1/2 tsp. salt
    1 tsp. baking soda

Add cocoa mixture. Add and mix well:
    1 c. water
    2 eggs
    3/4 c. buttermilk (can use dried, reconstituted)
    1 tsp. vanilla

Pour into pan and bake for 25 minutes. Five minutes before cake is done, make icing. Whip together:
    1 stick softened butter
    3 T cocoa
    6 T water
    1 tsp. vanilla
    1 box sifted powder sugar

Pour over cake as you take it from the oven (also OK if you wait till cake cools). Can cut into small pieces when cool, or freeze. To freeze: put in freezer for an hour or two. Cover top with cling wrap, then wrap with aluminum foil. Remove from freezer as you head for retreat. At the hospitality suite, remove foil and clear wrap. Cut into small pieces (a little goes a long way). Loosely cover with foil. Decoratively arrange on paper plates.

Chewy Noels

Melt and divide between two 9 x 13 pans
   1 stick butter

In a bowl, beat together
   8 eggs
   4 t. vanilla

Mix and add:
   4 c. dark brown sugar
   1 1/4 c. flour
   1/2 tsp. baking soda
   1 tsp. salt
   4 c. chopped pecans

Blend well, then pour into pans. Bake at 350° for 25 minutes or until firm to the touch. IMMEDIATELY turn out of pans onto cutting boards. Dust tops with powdered sugar. Cut these extremely rich goodies into small squares. Put them into tins. They'll keep a week or more. Don't forget to take them with you!

Checklist

It might be helpful to have a checklist so you'll cover all the bases:

Hospitality Bags

(Make it appropriate for the area!)

(Who can donate items?)

Bags

Tissue

Bottled water

Snack food (pretzels, crackers, raisins, orange, small candy bars, gum)

Antacid tablets

Written materials (guides, welcome letter, schedule, maps, etc.)

Volunteers to make them:

Who will deliver to facility:

How will participants get them? (front desk? delivered to rooms?)

ONE-DAY RETREAT

Breakfast

Juice (Tomato, cranberry, grapefruit, orange)

   and/or

Cut-up fruit

Bagels and cream cheese (regular and lite)

   and/or

Pastries (Danish, muffins, coffee cake)

Coffee (regular and decaf, sugar, cream – not white powder! – sweetener, pink and blue)

Soft drinks (regular and diet, including decaf) and bottled water

Mid-morning Snack

Coffee refreshed

Soft drinks and water replenished

Pretzels, or breakfast remainders

Lunch Buffet

Meat and cheese trays

Bread and rolls

Relishes and condiments

Vegetarian pasta

Salad or crudités or hot vegetable

Cookies or brownies

Mid-afternoon Snack

Coffee and Soft drinks

Pretzels

Cookies

Facility

Name:

Address:

Phone number:

Contact Person:

Directions (locally, or from airport):

Menu and per person cost requested

Meals

Snacks

Can we bring in our own food or drink?

Hospitality suite (can it be gratis?)

MULTI-DAY RETREAT

Hospitality Bags (see above)

Cocktail Hour

Wine or sherry

Nuts and chips

Opening Meal

Wine

Salad or soup

Chicken, beef or fish

Starch

Vegetable

Dessert

Evening Liqueurs?

1st Night

As above

Middle Night

On own

Last Night

Casual

Final Day Lunch

Get a count. Many will leave early.

Summing It Up

You've got the board retreat scheduled, you were unanimously selected as the food organizer and – bam! – you are now officially an expert. You will plan a fun, meaningful, tasty gustatory experience that participants will applaud you for. The facilitator will keep them on their mental toes; YOU will keep them nourished, energetic and performing at their peak. We hope you have fun yourself. No matter how serious is the business you will be conducting, the warmth of thoughtful concern, hearty laughter and yummy food always make an event memorable, the work manageable. Enjoy.

Rose Jonas, Ph.D.

Having a quiet cup of coffee with Rose Jonas in St. Louis is almost impossible. On the celebrity scale, it's more like hanging out with Dear Abby than Jennifer Lopez. Everyone needs a word of advice. Folks who don't know her from her 20 years of facilitating seminars, workshops and retreats, and being the mom of a high school senior and Ed Finkelstein's trophy wife, know her from her weekly appearance on the NBC-TV St. Louis affiliate where she's known as "The Job Doctor."

Rose has three specialties: 1. Managing the group process, which she does for clients and teaches in a graduate class at Washington University in St. Louis 2. Working with folks who are in career transition and 3. Becoming a famous author. She's written: *The Campaign that Couldn't Be Won* (about a school board election), *Can I Lie on My Resume: Strategies That Win the Career Game*, and is currently at work with Ellen Sweets on a cooking memoir: *Fast Friends, Fragrant Kitchens.*

Rose has a checkered past. Rose has earned her strength of character as well as great tenacity from being raised in a Catholic orphanage. She acquired insight into the pink-collar jungle during her 7 years as a legal secretary, while attending college at night. Rose learned about corporate life at Monsanto as a human resources director for 7 years. She nurtured her love of the limelight when she performed with the touring company of "The Sound of Music," where she was riveting as a postulant. She learned her way around a press release as a theatrical publicist representing Warner Brothers and the Royal Shakespeare Company.

Most recently, she has become a member of "The Chafing Dishes," an elite group of plus sized runners. Rose, who is incredibly pleasant when not exercising, is known as "Grumpy Spice."

Rose Jonas, Ph.D.
7600 Carswold
Clayton, MO 63105
314-863-1166
E-mail: JobDoc@aol.com

Ellen Sweets

If you want to have a fabulous night of great conversation, terrific food and just the right wine, Ellen Sweets is your woman. But don't even think of going on Monday. According to Ellen, everything is left over from the weekend and simply not up to par.

Ellen gained her great love of cuisine from growing up in a food and fun loving home where she cooked with her Father and Mother. Her Grandfather built his own barbecue pit with just the right distance between the meat and the heat. Food was serious business in the Sweets home.

Ellen started her professional life as a writer for her Father's newspaper, the *St. Louis American*. She moved from there to the *St. Louis Post-Dispatch* where she was a feature writer.

Ellen did a brief stint as the executive director of the St. Louis Civil Rights Enforcement Agency. True to her roots, her method of organizing always revolved around a great meal. Few could resist her charms!

She headed East to edit corporate publications for AT&T and to earn enough money to put her daughter Hannah Sweets through college at Shenandoah Conservatory. When Hannah quit college to become a professional dancer, Ellen quit the corporate world and went back to her first love, journalism. After performing professionally as a dancer for several years, Hannah gave up the dance and has become a chef. This coincided with Ellen's decision to write about food, where she launched the *Neiman Marcus Chef's Catalogue* website.

Ellen is currently living a mile high in Denver, where she is writing about her three favorite things: food, travel and people.

Ellen Sweets
303-820-1284
E-mail: EllenSweets@MSN.com

CHAPTER 5

Mission-Rich Icebreakers and Team-Building Exercises

Carol Weisman, MSW, CSP

G overnance is a team sport. Boards have to make difficult decisions. Members need to be able to discuss issues frankly. They need to know the skills of the other members when assigning work. And yet, unlike other teams, there is very little, if any, time spent on team building.

The board needs to focus on two things: the members and the mission. If a board can do this, it can get through almost anything. That is why retreats need to have a framework that will focus and clarify the mission, all while building interpersonal bonds. Obviously, many retreats are held to make strategic decisions, but without these two elements, the best decisions will not be made. This chapter explores some of the ways to use mission-rich icebreakers that produce results.

Board members are being asked to think more strategically and be less involved in tactics. This is the shift from management to governance. To do this, the board must have a clear understanding of what the mission of the charity is and how the agency fulfills it. To discuss these sometimes difficult and controversial subjects, board members need to know and trust each other.

An excellent example of this comes from the board of the Delta Center for Independent Living in St. Charles, MO. The board had been through two retreats when an extremely difficult issue arose: Should the Center permit clients to hire attendants who had failed a police background check?

Board members had very strong feelings. The board members who were disabled and used attendants believed that the consumer should make the decision. The nondisabled board members believed that the consumer and the center should be protected. Discussions were frank, impassioned, but always respectful. The board came to a compromise solution barring attendants who had been convicted of violent crimes. Thanks to a year of team building, the board was stronger than ever after this decision. Attendance at meetings was excellent and more people sought leadership opportunities.

Understand the Mission: Anyone who has ever been in sales knows that you can't sell what you don't understand. That's why many retreats are dedicated to explaining the mission to the board members. This is particularly important with complex organizations. For instance, an $8 million organization with 23 programs had a retreat where the major goal was to help board members understand the services that were offered to the community. Board members needed time outside of a regular board meeting to learn about their organization. Financial decisions were going to be made based on program needs, so the mission value of the programs had to be made clear. There was a constant Greek chorus of "I didn't know we do that."

Activities at a retreat must be chosen carefully. A friend of mine went to a retreat for the board of her undergraduate university. The facilitator chose outdoor team-building exercises involving a multi-colored parachute. It was a hot day. Participants were not told what kind of clothing to wear. The average age was 50. My friend was in her mid-60s. She had recently had back surgery. She was wearing pantyhose, heels and a linen suit. She was not wearing a smile.

After the parachute activity, she called for a cab, checked out of her hotel and went straight to the airport. Her comment to me was "There isn't enough money in my will for this university to make it worth their while to kill me off. They clearly don't care about me or my comfort and I'm caring less and less about them."

The staff of the university convinced my friend to come back the next year. They hired a new facilitator. They told the board to dress casually and asked members to bring photos of their college days. Instead of staying at an elegant hotel, they were housed at the dorm. The facilitator asked the board members to share their experiences of dormitory life. They ate pizza, popcorn and Hershey Bars while they relived both the good times and the challenges of being a college freshman.

Thanks to their night in the dormitory, the board was focused on university life. Before they left, one of the board members decided to endow a chair. He had been thinking of it for a long time, but this exercise focused the value of the education he had received.

My friend said of the second experience, "Thanks to the time spent in the dorm, I knew my fellow board members much better than before and actually made plans to see some of them during the year. And, I once again fell in love with my university. I felt excited, involved in and honored to be on the board." This is what can happen when the right exercises are chosen.

Choosing an Icebreaker:

Selecting the right activities to focus on the mission and team building requires planning and flexibility. I interview four groups before choosing an activity: staff, board leadership, emerging leaders and stinkers. I ask the staff and current leaders to identify emerging leaders and stinkers. Thomas Bakewell describes the interview process in his chapter. I also ask about the age and gender of the participants, the clothing they will be wearing, the diversity of the group, the facilities and any time constraints.

If you are in a boardroom and your activities will be done around a board table, it doesn't make much difference if board members are in suits, business casual or jeans, but if you want to do an outdoor activity or something messy, be sure to alert board members what they will need to wear to be comfortable and safe. For instance, while working with the Special Olympics, activities were planned which involved drawing on large sheets of paper on the floor. This icebreaker was chosen because some of the participants couldn't read. They were asked to draw their favorite Special Olympics Event either as a participant or a spectator. They were told to wear comfortable clothing. Drawing while sitting on the floor was both fun and different. It would have been a disaster for anyone in a favorite silk suit.

You need to be aware of the physical and cognitive challenges of the members. If you have board members who can't stand comfortably or are having other challenges, accommodations need to be made. For instance, when working with the Greater Los Angeles Association for the Deaf, we did activities that were focused so that the participants who needed to could see the person signing for me.

When choosing an icebreaker the facilitator also needs to respect the participant's need for personal space and distance. Consider giving an option when constructing an activity. For a mentoring program, you might want to ask, "Tell us about a time your parents or an adult in your life gave you terrific advice." For some people, their parents may never have given them great advice.

I do not believe that participants for most board retreats should be asked to touch one another. It implies an intimacy which exceeds the boundaries of most board interaction. There are always exceptions such as holding hands while saying Grace if this is a custom for a specific religious organization.

Always remember that icebreakers are meant to build teams not to break apart and shred boundaries. Creating comfort and trust will build commitment and understanding.

The Power of the Mission: I was once brought in to deal with two board members who had gotten into a fistfight during a previous meeting. We spent the first two hours of the discussion talking about why the mission of the organization was important not only to them, but to the entire community. They eventually decided that their personal differences were petty compared to the needs and values that the organization stood for and the services it provided. Although they didn't become best friends, these two women were willing and able to work together in future meetings.

Sometimes bringing the mission to the meeting is incredibly simple. For instance, if yours is a faith-based organization, start with a prayer or a scriptural reading that is relevant to the work you're doing. Another quick, simple, inexpensive way to focus on the mission is to put the mission statement on the back of name tents. The member's name goes on one side, and the mission statement faces the board member.

Bring a Client/Customer/Student or Patient to the Meeting:

The board will be able to hear the story of one who is served by the organization. There is one caveat: Because many organizations are dedicated to serving and protecting individuals, they cannot in good conscience exploit them in a meeting. Care must be taken to ensure that the person visiting the meeting really wants to attend and will be empowered by the experience, and will be a good example of what the organization hopes to achieve.

Examples:

1. The Women's Self Help Center board in St. Louis asked its therapists if there was a woman who had been through one of the programs who could explain the process to the board. The woman who spoke to them was an incest survivor in her early 50s. She told her story of abuse by a relative, then abuse to herself through alcohol and drugs. She talked about how she had found The Women's Self Help Center, and about her time in therapy. She said she felt like the retreat was her graduation exercise and thanked the board for letting her come.

2. Jewish Family Service of Rochester, NY, invited a family that had adopted a baby to address the board at its retreat. The Mom came with a beautiful, lively toddler and explained to the board how the agency's investment in this program had benefited the lives of everyone in her family. She talked about how her daughter was adopted from the same area of Russia that her family had immigrated from during the pogroms. The board unanimously said that the family's visit was the best part of the retreat.

Bring the Board to the Mission:

Advantages: The board can see and experience the site where a program takes place as well as observe changes, the need for improvements or ongoing projects. Sometimes sites are remote and inconvenient for members, but the benefits are worth the effort of making the trip.

1. The Sequoia Fund Board of Sequoia National Park had its retreat in the lodge at the top of the park. After getting to the park, board members had an hour drive through the magnificent sequoias, where they could leave their lives behind and focus on the beauty of the forest. There was an opportunity for board members to view new projects that needed funding and to explore areas that were being reclaimed.

2. The board president of a Boy Scout Council mentioned that as a child he had never been a scout. For the board retreat, he took members on a campout to experience what the children they serve were enjoying. When they sat around the campfire eating "s'mores" (a treat made of graham crackers, marshmallows and chocolate), the members were amazed to find that despite the fact that they were from different parts of the country, each knew someone who knew someone who was positive that when the teenagers came home, there was a hook on the door of the car!

When they returned to the city and their business suits, they found that they could disagree and discuss difficult matters with a spirit of respect and camaraderie.

Take a New Look at the Mission:

Photograph the mission: Send board members out with cameras to photograph the area they are protecting and improving. This takes several hours, and participants need to be near an outlet for one-hour photo processing.

1. The board members of a historic-preservation program were given single-use cameras and sent out to photograph the Main Street area. Each pair was assigned a specific architectural feature to capture. While the photographs were being developed, the participants had lunch and shared how differently they were able to see their town. For board members who were new to historic preservation, this was a marvelous introduction to appreciating what needed to be preserved.

2. An environmental organization concerned with pollution put photos of a contaminated site on the back of board member's name tents to focus the board on what they were trying to clean up.

Hear From the Other Board Members:

Ask board members to share their personal experiences with the mission. Pass a 3-minute timer so the session moves along. Keep in mind that with highly emotional issues, board members can feel put upon or exposed.

1. A mentoring program asked each of the board members to share an experience where mentoring had been helpful in their personal, professional or volunteer lives.

2. A board committed to supporting research to find a cure for breast cancer asked each member to talk about his or her experiences that led them to volunteer for this charity.

Have a Quiz:

Activity: Ask the staff to produce a quiz that reflects the areas you believe are important for the board to understand. For instance, the mission, the history, bylaws. Include some fun questions. This is a great activity to do in teams. Match up new board members with old. Give prizes. Consider having the same quiz at the next board meeting to check for retention.

Example: National Council on Alcohol and Drug Abuse Board, St. Louis, MO. BOARD QUIZ

1. NCADA first opened its doors in March, 19 _____ .

2. Today, NCADA serves St. Louis City and the following six surrounding counties:

    √ _____

    √ _____

    √ _____

    √ _____

    √ _____

    √ _____

3. NCADA annually serves approx. _____ individuals, including _____ youth.

4. Complete the NCADA tagline: *NCADA is the place to turn for prevention,* _____ , _____ , *public awareness, and advocacy.*

5. Name two things the RADAR grant funds:
   _____ and _____

6. What is the *HEROES* Campaign slogan?
   _____

   _____

7. TRUE or FALSE? *Only cash contributions of $100 or more may be eligible for Missouri's Youth Opportunities Program (YOP) tax credits.*

8. NCADA's Web site address is **www.** _____

9. What do the acronyms **RTI** and **TREND** stand for?

    RTI: _____

    TREND: _____

10. Within $50,000, what is the 2001 budget? $ _____

11. What anniversary will the 2002 Golf Tournament celebrate and which present illustrious board president introduced the Tournament? _____ **th anniversary**

    initiated by _____

12. How long has Ed Tasch served as executive director? _____

BONUS: Write the NCADA mission statement as revised and approved in 2000.

Celebrate Victories:

Activity: Ask each board member to share what they are celebrating in their personal, business or volunteer life. This can be a powerful activity when the work of the organization is overwhelming. Many nonprofits do not take the time to celebrate progress. This sets a positive tone for the whole meeting. At the end of the retreat, ask board members and staff what they would like to celebrate next year at this time.

Example: One board I worked with was having trouble meeting goals with a capital campaign. We began by asking members to celebrate victories in their personal, professional or volunteer life. The first person said that the month before he had been diagnosed with prostate cancer and he was celebrating that it was contained and he expected a full cure. No one on the board was aware of this. Others shared surprising personal victories including reconciliation with family, weight loss, a pay raise, a child's academic achievement. After this exercise, board members were in a positive place to deal with the fiscal mess they were in. For the first time, there was a willingness to take personal responsibility for work not completed.

Bring in the Founder:

Activity: Many organizations have rich histories that are never fully explored by board members. Some founders are still alive and can share their story in person. Bring them to the meeting. Be sure to incorporate time for questions and answers.

When the founder is long-deceased, consider asking a local acting group if it would like to put on a short play about how the organization was founded.

Example: Guardian Angel Settlement House in St. Louis invited the religious founders of the Daughters of Charity to visit from the 17th century. The board was led into the dimly lit chapel before dinner to meet the founders. St. Vincent de Paul discussed his ability to partner with the rich to help the poor, which was an obvious parallel to the work of the board. After St. Vincent de Paul and St. Louise de Mariac told about their lives and the founding of the order, a lively question-and-answer period followed. Few forgot how and why the order had been founded.

Bring in an Outside Expert:

Activity: Every board member brings specific expertise to an organization, but sometimes they lack a few of an entire industry. Bringing an expert with a mile-high view can help decision-makers on the ground. When choosing an expert, look for someone with both knowledge and the ability to describe an industry or challenge in laymen's terms.

Example: Beauvais Manor on the Park is an assisted-living residential center in St. Louis. To begin the visioning process, Ann Bannes, a geriatric planning expert from St. Andrew's At-Home Services described how Americans are aging, what their future needs will be and how the "Baby Boomers" approach to aging differs from the current elderly population.

Summary:

The work of the board is to make strategic decisions. To do this, board members have to know, respect and trust fellow board members. A retreat is a marvelous opportunity to build that trust and focus on the mission. Activities that are relevant and reflect the physical, intellectual and emotional needs and abilities of the group will create an environment where learning and solid decision-making will flourish.

Carol Weisman, MSW, CSP

Carol Weisman, president of Board Builders, is a speaker, author, trainer and consultant who specializes in volunteerism, fund raising and governance. Ms. Weisman has a Master's Degree is Social Work and a Masters Degree in Education from Washington University in St. Louis. She has served on 25 boards and has been president of 7.

Carol has worked as a medical social worker in pediatric oncology, hematology and neurology and neurosurgery at St. Louis Children's Hospital and Children's Hospital National Medical Center. She has published extensively on governance and volunteerism and is the author of *Build a Better Board in 30 Days: A Practical Guide for Busy Trustees* published by the F. E. Robbins and Sons Press. She is also featured in the PBS/Learning Institute Program on "Building a Board with a Passion for Mission."

In addition to traveling the world giving keynotes, training and doing board retreats, Carol is a member of the board of the Gateway Chapter of the National Speaker's Association. She serves on the Board of the Sequoia National Park Foundation.

Carol lives with her sweet, long suffering husband of 26 years. Their oldest son Frank Robbins V lives in New York where he is an actor by night and an aspiring real estate mogul during the day. Their other son Jono Robbins just finished art school with a major in ceramics and glass blowing and is starting to look for a teaching position. The dog and cat are long gone, and Carol is thinking of letting the plants die.

Carol Weisman, MSW, CSP
Board Builders, Inc.
48 Granada Way, St. Louis, MO 63124
phone: 888-500-1777 (toll free) • FAX: 314-991-0202
E-mail: carol@boardbuilders.com
www.boardbuilders.com

CHAPTER 6

Establishing Ground Rules

Kristin J. Arnold, CMC, CPF, CSP

N on-profit boards have unique personalities. Some characteristics you cherish; others drive you crazy. Whether you realize it or not, your board is operating under a certain set of implicit "ground rules" that reinforce specific behaviors. Some you like; some you don't.

To reinforce desired behaviors and extinguish undesirable behaviors, the annual board retreat is a perfect time and place to establish your Board's "ground rules." Ground rules are explicit agreements on how the Board will function. They clearly articulate boundaries of appropriate behavior. For example, are you tired of having your Board members come ill-prepared? Don't know what to do when one person dominates? Effective ground rules *prevent* these undesirable behaviors from happening in the first place. They also create a space to *intervene* – reminding each other of agreements made to each other.

As you formulate your ground rules, consider how your Board will deal with common concerns such as:

- **Interruptions.** What to do when board members are called out of the meeting. How will you deal with phone calls and messages. Will pager and cellular phones be tolerated?

- **Assignments.** If board members cannot fulfill their obligations, who should they notify and by when?

- **Substitutions.** In the event a board member can't make it to the meeting, are "substitutions" allowed? How will the Board's work be communicated to the missing Board member?

- **Decisions.** Will you use Roberts Rules of Order or a less formal process? How will the Board make decisions? Are the team members aiming for consensus? Is there a "fallback" in case the team can't come to a consensus? Is the Board President ultimately responsible for making the decision?

- **Confidentiality.** Are there topics or kinds of information that should not be discussed outside the Board?

- **Penalties.** How will the Board deal with minor and chronic violations to the ground rules?

Ground rules are simply the glue that holds the team together. Here's an example of one Board's ground rules:

- **Honor time limits.** Be on time. Start on time. End on time. Set a time frame for each deliverable. Do your part to meet individual and Board commitments.

- **All participate...no one dominates.** Ask for ideas from everyone. Recognize and consider others' ideas. Accept all suggestions as valid for consideration.

- **Work together.** Board members communicate and work closely together and make every effort to support one another. Keep each other informed. Work together to solve problems. Offer help without being asked.

- **Listen as allies.** Give your undivided attention to the person speaking. Seek first to understand, then to be understood. Respect each other by not interrupting. Stay on track. Stick to the subject at hand. Minimize distractions and needless debate.

- **Be considerate.** Consider the background, motivations and skills of other Board members when offering help or advice. Be open to constructive feedback.

- **Celebrate small successes.** Recognize team and individual effort. A lot.

- **Knock three times.** Simply knock your knuckle or a pen on the table three times if the discussion starts to wander or there is another minor violation of the ground rules. Whoever is speaking should stop and refocus on the topic.

- **Respect time and each other.**

It all boils down to this one last ground rule: respect one another. Unfortunately, many boards don't spend enough time together to really get to know each other – and develop a level of trust or respect. So it's important to create an open climate to allow people to get to know each other over their specific term.

Telephone Conference Calls

Ground rules are particularly effective when conducting meetings over the phone. Telephone conference calls are a low cost alternative for board members to meet while physically located in different places. They are great for routine status reports and for short-term, problem solving meetings – but not if you follow your instincts to just grab the phone and start talking! Conference calls are not as easy as a one-on-one phone conversations, so follow these tips or ground rules for effective conference calls:

- **Use a moderator.** One person (typically the person who initiated the call) should be the moderator. Start with a "roll call" of attendees and their location so that everyone knows who is on the line and announce when new members join in. Give a short, precise overview of the purpose and goal of the call, followed by a simple, clear agenda. Ask the participants to follow the agenda and conference call ground rules.

- **Keep up the pace.** Most people usually speak very slowly, careful of what they say and how they say it. But the average person is able to decode verbal information four to five times faster than the average speaking rate. This makes for a very long, tedious meeting! The moderator should set the tone of the conference call by speaking at a regular rate with good inflection and intensity. Other participants will then follow the leader in style and rate. The moderator should also ask the participants to limit their contributions to a reasonable length (for example one or one and a half minutes) and allow questions for clarification.

- **Manage voice traffic.** The more people you have on the line, the greater the potential for overload and domination of a few people. Limit the number of people involved in the conference call to board members and one or two scheduled speakers. Ask the participants to state their names and location each time they speak. Recognize that one individual at one location will have more "air time" than several people huddled around a speaker phone at another location. If possible, questions should be directed to specific individuals; for example, "John, will you share your perspective on this issue?" or "Mary, could you please clarify that issue?" The moderator may serve as a "gatekeeper" to ensure everyone has the opportunity to participate.

- **Take a poll.** At critical moments in the meeting, poll the participants for their input. Call out each name and ask for their opinion, comment or vote. Recognize that this will take time, especially for larger groups, but is worthwhile for critical issues where the team must make a decision to move forward.

- **Use handouts.** Where possible, mail or fax information to be used during the conference call. Quantifiable data such as sales forecasts, trend charts, and other descriptive data is helpful to have prior to the meeting so that everyone is looking at and commenting on the same information.

Phone conference calls can save time, travel costs, energy and hassle – especially if the Board follows these basic ground rules to enhance the effectiveness of your next conference call.

Email Communications

In addition to conference calls, electronic mail or "email" has the enormous potential for enabling, as well as complicating, the ways we communicate. Spend a few moments thinking about how best to communicate among board members using email:

- **Check your inbox.** Agree on how often board members will check messages. For example, if in the office, we agree to check our inbox first thing in the morning, at lunch and before we leave for the day. While traveling, we agree to check our email at least once a day. Agree on a reasonable time to respond to incoming email – typically within one working day.

- **Know your limits.** Know each other's technical limitations and capabilities. Some have high-speed access and instant email notification. Others, especially those emailing from home, may have technical limitations that effect how quickly they can receive or respond.

- **Be tolerant** of your fellow board members' mistakes. Some are new to using email correctly, so be gracious. Coach them. Support them. Give helpful feedback and suggestions. On the other hand, don't be shy, either. Ask others for help and learn how to use email its fullest and best potential. Accept the inevitable communication errors. Apologize and clarify the misunderstanding. Be gracious and learn from your mistakes.

- **Be easy.** Increase your ease with the keyboard. Learn how to type at least 50 words per minute using inexpensive typing tutor programs such as *Mavis Beacon Teaches Typing*. Learn your software's speed keys to navigate quickly through your email program.

- **Email with integrity.** Get back to Board members when you say you will. Team members will assume the worst if they don't hear from you. Prevent their imaginations from conjuring up wild stories by letting them know you received the email and are still working on it.

- **Limit the excess.** Agree on when it is appropriate to send a "paper copy" versus an email. Do not send a paper copy AND an email. Do one or the other; not both. Avoid back and forth replies such as "thank you" and "okay." You don't have to acknowledge each and every email.

- **Be sensitive.** Agree on how to pass along critical information. Sometimes, email is NOT the preferred medium. Do not hide behind email to say something you should say face to face (F2F). Agree on what is acceptable and unacceptable information to be passed by email. If you must email confidential information, agree to write "confidential" in the subject line. Otherwise, after multiple replies, the confidentiality will be long lost or forgotten.

- **Don't flame others.** Flaming emails (strongly worded, emotionally charged opinions) destroy teamwork. Avoid *pit-bull* phrases such as "That's a stupid idea." (opinionated declarations); "I'm not about to…" (heated denials); "Why is everyone…" (paranoid remarks). Don't respond to incoming flames by email, otherwise, you will be entering into an "email flame war" where no one emerges victorious. Instead, go face to face (F2F) or pick up the phone.

- **Stop "urban legends."** These requests to forward letters to [help a dying child], [save the planet], [cause of the day] are often unknowingly forwarded by kind-hearted, politically conscious board members. Don't be fooled into thinking it's safe because you know the person sending it. Check out its validity at www.urbanlegends.com. Or better yet, don't send it on to others.

- **Check your privacy.** Review your company *and* organization policy on email and Internet use. Understand that email is about as private as a postcard. You essentially have no right to privacy. Your email lives on long after you have hit the Delete button.

- **Agree on common abbreviations** (or acronyms) such as *As Soon As Possible* (ASAP), *For Your Information* (FYI), *Close* *of Business* (COB), *By The Way* (BTW) and *In My Opinion* (IMO). A good rule of thumb is to only use acronyms common to the English language, your industry, your team product/project, or your organizational culture.

- **Use smileys sparingly.** Emoticons or "smileys" haven't hit mainstream email yet; however, they can help board members distinguish the tone of a message. Discuss the advantages and disadvantages of using emoticons and agree on when and how they should be used effectively.

- **Set up a distribution list.** To make it easy to send a message to all board members, set up a distribution list that automatically sends a message to a predetermined list of people.

- **Attach documents.** Agree on attachment specifications such as type and version of software. Include any compression software and settings, if applicable.

- **Be considerate** of others when communicating by email. When writing an email, remember that your email is *one of many other emails* that land in the inbox. Make it easy for others to read and respond to your messages quickly.

Email works best for short bursts of information, especially if it needs to be communicated among several or all board members. If you find you have been bouncing emails on the same subject three or more times, pick up the phone and talk directly with the person.

Establish Ground Rules

Set aside some time during your board's annual planning retreat to discuss and agree on your ground rules. The best time on the agenda is usually after the preliminary issues (e.g., organizational mission, short and long term goals, board staff relations and other strategic issues). Ask a well-respected, "people person" to facilitate ground rule development – don't feel like you have to "do it all." Get others involved to create a greater sense of "team."

To establish your ground rules, follow these four steps:

First, have an overall discussion of what ground rules are and the importance of following the ground rules.

Second, ask the board members for potential ground rules. Don't forget to capture the answers on a flipchart or projected visual so all can see what is proposed. There are several ways to gather a list of potential ground rules:

If the board is familiar with the concept, simply ask the board a direct question, "What ground rules would you like to have in place to ensure smooth teamwork?"

Put together a list of suggested ground rules (culled from this article and/or from your personal experiences). Ask the board members to read through the suggested ground rules and ask for agreement and/or modifications. (Beware: this is the quickest method, but will have the least amount of buy-in because it is, after all, your list!)

Stimulate thinking by asking an indirect question, capturing the answers into potential ground rules. For example, ask:

From your experience, what makes a great board versus a non-effective board?

What are your expectations of each other? How do we expect to operate as a team?

How do we expect our organization to treat our customers?

If the organization has defined the "values," take each value and ask, "What does this mean to us?" What kinds of behaviors would promote this value?"

Third, go through each item and ask, "Can we agree to this?" If someone cannot agree, ask, "What is it you cannot agree to?" Combine similar ideas into a final, agreed-upon list.

Finally, make sure the team agrees on the entire list and commits to follow the ground rules. If there seems to be many ground rules that need to be "cleaned up," merged or massaged, as a small group to work on the ground rules and present it to the entire board at the next meeting.

Enforce Ground Rules

Once ground rules have been established, discuss how the Board will enforce the ground rules. It may be enough to read the list a the start of each meeting, or you may want board members to provide one another with a "constructive reminder." Some teams use the "three knock rule" – knock three times when you see team member breaking a ground rule. Others use a "penalty pot," to which each team member contributes a penny, nickel or quarter for each violation of a ground rule. At then end of the year, the board decides what to do with the money. (A warning: some boards really get into using the penalty pot as a an excuse to break the ground rules!)

Don't be surprised if the ground rules don't appear to "stick" right off the bat. All teams progress through a typical pattern of development. Initially, board members will be too polite to point out infractions of the ground rules. Initially, you will have to rely on personal accountability.

After the board has been working with each other for a while, they will feel more comfortable to call each other on their behavior. They will add new, more meaningful ground rules, and the less significant ground rules will slide off the list (usually because the Board doesn't have a problem with them any more!). Also, when the new members come on board, you'll have to let them know up front what the ground rules are – explicit expectations of how the Board will work cooperatively together and how they will manage the inevitable conflicts.

Keep in mind, the typical board comes together once a month or once a quarter to grapple with sometimes difficult decisions for a mission they believe in – often quite passionately. They may, in fact, have little or not tolerance to build a relationship with their fellow board members, no less build a sense of "team." However, as a key leader, you must foster that sense of teamwork. Without the relations, mutual trust and respect, you board will not be as effective as it can be.

Ground rules are to teams as the Constitution of the United States is to America. Ground rules provide a solid foundation to the values of the Board. They clearly state what is important to the team and what board members can expect from each other. As the board evolves and matures, the ground rules will change, creating "amendments" to the Board's constitution.

Kristin J. Arnold, CMC, CPF, CSP

Kristin was one of the first women graduates from the Coast Guard Academy and was the first woman aboard the Coast Guard Cutter Buttonwood out of Galveston, Texas. When asked why the Coast Guard, she answered "I wanted to do something different from everyone else."

When everyone else was playing with Barbies, Kristin was playing handball with anyone who wanted to play.

As the youngest of four children, she had the freedom to find her own way. When she decided to apply for the Coast Guard Academy, her Father was totally mystified; her mother thought it was cool. When she sent home the photo of herself with her buzz cut, it was her Father who cried. Her mother lived vicariously through Kristin's adventures.

Kristin graduated with honors from the United States Coast Guard Academy. She also earned a Master of Business Administration degree, with an emphasis on Marketing Strategy, from St. Mary's College in California, again graduating with high honors. With eleven years on active duty in the Coast Guard both underway and ashore, Kristin learned firsthand what it takes to be an extraordinary team.

Travis, her first child was born at Naval Hospital Oakland weighing in at only 1 pound and 2 ounces. Needless to say, the first three years were very difficult. But the good news is that Travis is a healthy, happy, typical teenager. In 1992, when her daughter Marina was one year old, Kristin launched Quality Process Consultants, Inc. It is the team building and the planning skills that give her the basis to build a quality consulting firm.

Kristin is a CPF (Certified Professional Facilitator), a CSP (Certified Speaking Professional) and a CMC (Certified Management Consultant). She tried to put more acronyms behind her name, but it started looking like a jigsaw puzzle. Kristin also trains other facilitators. When asked what she does, Kristin states *"I train your people to do what I do – facilitate teams to higher levels of performance."*

Kristin J. Arnold
Quality Process Consultants, Inc.
11304 Megan Drive, Fairfax, VA 22030-5510
800-589-4733 or 703-278-0892
www.qpcteam.com

CHAPTER 7

Retreats to Prepare Mission and Vision Statements

John M. Bryson, Ph.D.
and
Barbara C. Crosby, Ph.D.

I t is easy to justify spending organizational resources on a retreat to produce something as vital to an organization's success as a compelling, inspiring mission and vision statement. A well-designed retreat for this purpose will be what Evans and Boyte (1986) call a "free space," or what we call an "island of the imagination" (cf. Holm, 2000, 329-336). These are spaces in which a group of people can summon and give voice to the soul and spirit of their organization. As Holm says, "The imagination is the only divine spark in us – kill it, and you kill any possibility of growing a soul" (2000, 331).

Yet, not every time is right for such a retreat. If your organization is in the midst of a crisis or riven by internal dissent, you may need to respond to immediate needs before bringing everyone together to focus on vision and mission. On the other hand, if the organization is about to undertake a change in top leadership, the organization's board may wish to reassess the mission and vision in order to help understand what type of leader the organization needs, rather than expect a new leader to make any necessary changes in overall direction.

Assuming the time is right, mission and vision retreats can have substantial payoffs. This chapter will describe the benefits of holding retreats when the time is right to create or revisit mission and vision statements. Attention will be given to planning and conducting productive retreats that include the right players. Included will be advice on laying the necessary groundwork for these retreats and for ensuring that the work of the retreat has real impact on the organization.

Mission and Vision Defined

Before going further, it is helpful to define mission and vision statements. An organization's **mission statement** is "an action-oriented formulation of the organization's reason for existence" (Bryson and Alston, 1994, 44). It encapsulates the organization's sense of direction and purpose in relation to its stakeholders. The mission statements of four nonprofit organizations are presented in Table 1.

A mission statement should be a continuous reference point, a reminder to internal and external stakeholders of what the organization is all about. To be effective, the statement should be brief and possess "breadth, durability, challenge, and distinction" (Angelica, 2001, 6). Often a mission statement is distilled into a memorable slogan or rallying cry that can roll easily off everyone's tongue (Angelica, 2001, 5). For example, the Humphrey Institute's mission has often been distilled into "Education for Public Responsibility." Westminster Presbyterian's slogan is "A Telling Presence in the City."

A **vision statement** should clearly and succinctly describe what the organization "should look like after it successfully implements its strategies and achieves its full potential" (Bryson, 1995, 155). In other words, it captures the organization's "desired future" (Angelica, 2001, 7). Vision statements will vary in their completeness and detail, ranging from a "vision sketch" to a full-blown "vision of success" that incorporates the organization's mission, core philosophy, goals, basic strategies, performance criteria, key decision-making rules, and ethical standards (Bryson, 1995, 155-165). A sketch may be all that is needed to guide strategy formulation, while a fuller, more complete vision can provide necessary guidance for strategy implementation. Of course, a vision statement does not have to consist of words. For example, Medtronic, a Minnesota corporation that manufactures heart pacemakers and other medical devices, effectively communicates its vision with an artistic logo that shows a person rising from a prone to an upright, healthy position. The

Table 1. Sample Mission Statements for Four Nonprofit Organizations

Organization and Location	Mission Statement
Courage Center Golden Valley, MN http://www.courage.org	The mission of **Courage Center** is to empower people with physical disabilities to reach for their full potential in every aspect of life.
Amherst H. Wilder Foundation St. Paul, MN http://www.wilder.org	Since 1906, the **Amherst H. Wilder Foundation** has been committed to: ...relieve, aid and assist the poor, sick and needy people of the city of Saint Paul...by all appropriate means...without regard to their nationality, place of residence, sex, color, or religious prejudices.
Westminster Presbyterian Church Minneapolis, MN http://www.wpc-mpls.org	In response to the grace of God through Jesus Christ, the mission of **Westminster Presbyterian Church** is: • To proclaim and celebrate the Good News of Jesus; • To gather as an open community to worship God with dignity and joy, warmth and beauty; • To nourish personal faith and commitment through study, prayer and fellowship; • To be a welcoming and caring Christian community witnessing to God's love day by day; • To work locally and beyond with our denomination and the larger Christian church; and • To be a telling presence in the city.
Hubert H. Humphrey Institute of Public Affairs University of Minnesota Minneapolis, MN http://www.hhh.umn.edu	The mission of the **Hubert H. Humphrey Institute of Public Affairs** is to prepare leaders for public work and to design and evaluate institutions of governance that accomplish public purposes.

idea graphically depicts the corporation's vision of "restoring people to health" (see http://www.medtronic.com).

Courage Center offers an example of a short vision statement: "We are guided by the vision that one day, all people will live, work, learn and play in a community based on abilities not disabilities" (http://www.courage.org).

Benefits of Creating (and Re-Creating) Mission and Vision Statements

The most important benefit of bringing people together to create or review an organizational **mission statement** is that it "fosters a habit of focusing discussion on what is truly important" (Bryson 1995, 68). Other benefits are:

- Attention to the organization's stakeholders
- Clarification of the organization's purpose
- Clarification of the purpose of organizational structures and systems
- Assistance in managing internal conflict
- Promotion of behavior that benefits the organization
- Explicit attention to philosophy, values, and culture

Further explanation of these benefits may be found in Bryson, 1995, 68-70.

An inspiring, achievable **vision of success** can be a powerful motivator and guide. Its benefits include:

- Specific, reasonable, supportive guidance about what behavior is expected within the organization
- Enhanced capacity of organizational members to discriminate between actions that will or will not contribute to desired outcomes
- An affirmation of the desired future
- A "useful tension between the world as it is and the world as we would like it" (Bryson, 1995, p. 158)

- A sense among organizational members of being "called" to virtuous, significant work
- Recognition of barriers to achieving the vision
- Significant reduction in organizational conflict
- Organizational capacity to deal with crises
- An internal and external image of organizational virtue and progress

Further explanation of these benefits may be found in Bryson, 1995, 157-159.

Types of Mission and Vision Retreats

The creation or re-creation of mission and vision statements may or may not be part of a strategic planning process. Organizations that are not engaged in strategic planning can certainly benefit from bringing people together to articulate the organization's mission and clarify its vision in light of stakeholder expectations and organizational mandates. Retreats that prompt organizational members to focus on mission and vision may be helpful during the organization's formative period and at multi-year intervals after that (Angelica, 2001, 11-12).

Organizations that are beginning a strategic planning process generally will want to pay attention to developing a mission statement early in the process. They may also choose to create a "vision sketch" to help guide strategy formulation. A full-blown "vision of success" typically should come after such organizations are well along in the process – that is, after they have developed a clear set of goals and strategies that they wish to implement. The vision of success then becomes a guide for strategy implementation (Bryson and Alston, 1996, p. 91).

Once an organization has developed a strategic plan and accompanying vision statement, the organizational mission and vision can be reviewed annually as part of a regular update of the strategic plan. Every few years, a full-blown revamping of the plan will probably be needed, and that may be the occasion for holding retreats to work on the mission and vision statements.

Desired Outcomes of Mission and Vision Retreats

The most obvious tangible desired outcome of a retreat aimed at creating an organizational mission is a draft mission statement. It is important to include the word draft, since not all organizational members are likely to be at the retreat, and it will be important to give them a chance to respond to the draft. Even the retreat participants may come up with some improvements to the statement if they have a chance to mull it over for a few days afterward. Other outcomes are:

- An inclusive list of stakeholders and their expectations of the organization
- A statement of organizational values
- Shared commitments to "real-ize" the mission
- Renewed stakeholder support for the organization

A retreat aimed at developing organizational vision should produce a potent vision statement, in words or other symbols. If the vision is to be translated into a full-blown "vision of success," the retreat should produce a draft statement that includes mission, basic philosophy and core values, goals, basic strategies, performance criteria, key decision-making rules, and ethical standards.

In addition to tangible desired outcomes, several intangible outcomes are important. When mission and vision retreats work well, they also enhance organizational relationships and morale. They heighten commitment to shared work and build enthusiasm for working toward future goals (Friend and Hickling, 1997, 98-103).

It is important to acknowledge that participants may be skeptical about the value of the retreat because they think it will be a waste of time or that nothing will come of it. In other words, participants may fear that none of the desired outcomes listed above are likely to be achieved. Particularly worrying are fears that the organizational culture or power dynamics will undermine any efforts to renew or revise the mission or vision in practice. A common fear is that the organization's positional leaders may publicly espouse a fine-sounding mission and vision, but everyone knows that the organization's day-to-day operation has little to do with either. Or, the organizational makeup and culture may be highly fragmented. Stakeholders may be unable to agree on mission and vision in any but the most abstract terms. In addition, organizational politics may be an issue. Participants may be enmeshed in internal power struggles, and the people who feel that they are losing out or on the margins will see such a retreat as one more opportunity for the most powerful group to impose their views on everyone else. In such cases the people in leadership roles may need to provide evidence that they are committed to acting on the results of the retreat, or that the culture and power dynamics, if not changing, at least are recognized as issues. It is particularly important to note that in situations that are fraught, retreat planners may need to take special care that all participants in the retreat have a safe way to voice their ideas and views without fear of retaliation.

Who Participates

In the best case, everyone in the organization will participate in a retreat to craft something as important as the organizational mission and vision statements. If the organization is quite large, however, considerable resources may be needed to bring everyone together. Large organizations may want to use some form of large-group interaction method to conduct the retreat (Bryson and Anderson, 2000; Holman and Devane, 1999).

The retreat design to be presented here should work well for small to medium-sized organizations (say, 50 members) or for large organizations that choose to involve some subset of the organization. The more people involved, the more time it is likely to take to work through the retreat agenda.

The subset may be the board of directors, the staff, the top management team, a group that represents the different departments and levels of the organization, an advisory board, or "customers." In general, it is best to assemble a representative group so there will be input and buy-in from throughout the organization. Sometimes, however, a board of directors may be the best participants – as, for example, when the organization is in the process of being formed and only the board exists, or when the board revisits the mission and vision as part of hiring a new executive director. Sometimes it may make sense to have just the top management team involved. For example, it may be that basic strategies clearly are not working, need to be rethought, and major realignments are likely to be necessary in which many existing staff will have to be laid off. Prior to such a drastic set of moves, it makes excellent sense to revisit the mission and vision statements in order to figure out if and how to involve the board and, if possible, the staff in re-assessing the mission, vision, or strategies. If a non-representative group is involved – such as the board – retreat organizers will be wise to consult people from throughout the organization in preparation for the retreat and they must include time on the agenda to plan for widely circulating the draft mission and vision statements and responding to comments.

In many cases, retreat organizers may want to invite people from outside the organization to participate in the retreat. Representatives of the organization's key customers or funders, for example, may be helpful in clarifying what these groups need and expect from the organization. At the very least, key stakeholder groups probably should be consulted in preparation for the retreat.

It is also possible that a unit within a larger organization will plan a retreat to consider its specific mission and vision within the context of the larger organization's mission. The retreat organizers should consult key stakeholders in other parts of the organization as well as external stakeholders in planning the retreat.

Agenda and Guidelines for a Mission/Vision Retreat

An agenda and guidelines will be presented for a single one-day retreat aimed at creating or reviewing a mission statement and a "sketch" vision statement. The larger the group at the retreat, the more likely an additional half or full day will be needed to work through the agenda. See Table 2.

The agenda items are discussed in more detail on the following page. Guidance for developing or reviewing a full-blown vision of success can be found in Bryson and Alston, 1996, 91-95, and Angelica, 2001, 25-35.

Table 2. Sample Agenda for a One-Day Mission and Vision Retreat for a Group of Twelve

Time	Topic
Pre-Retreat	Preparation
8:00 – 8:30 am	Registration and Coffee
8:30 – 9:00 am	Introduction • Purpose and Desired Outcomes of Retreat • People Involved • Hopes and Fears Exercise, or Light-Hearted Ice-breaker • Ground Rules
9:00 – 10:00 am	Stakeholder Analysis
10:00 – 10:30 am	Break (coffee, tea, juices, water, fresh fruit, pastry; go for a walk)
10:30 – 11:00 am	Mandates – what the organization must do, as required by law, regulations, charter, etc.
11:00 – Noon	Organizational Highs and Lows
Noon – 1:00 pm	Lunch
1:00 – 2:30 pm	Mission Elements
2:30 – 3:00 pm	Break (coffee, tea, juices, water, fresh fruit, cookies; go for a walk)
3:00 – 4:30 pm	Strategy Analysis
4:30 – 5:30 pm	Break (coffee, tea, juices, water, fresh fruit, cookies; go for a walk)
5:30 – 6:30 pm	Light Supper
6:30 – 8:00 pm	Vision Collage
8:00 – 8:30 pm	Action Steps • Decide review, adoption, and implementation process • Appoint drafting committee
8:30 pm	Adjournment
8:30 – 9:00 pm	Tying Up Loose Ends • Make sure all materials are collected • Drafting committee meets to decide how to proceed

PREPARATION

In a small organization, a single staff person may have the responsibility of organizing the retreat, but often a team is best for developing an over-all plan and parceling out tasks. The retreat plan should include:

- **Calendar** – Given the group we wish to involve, when should the retreat be scheduled in order to optimize participation? (Include consideration of work and family responsibilities, religious holidays, etc.) How much lead time will we need between announcing and conducting the retreat? Can we identify more than one possible date, so that we have more leeway in securing a site?

- **Selection of a site** – Is it affordable and physically accessible? Will it provide a relaxing environment and good refreshments or meals? Can participants' dietary desires and restrictions be accommodated? Is the site welcoming to all the participants? Are there spaces for breakout groups? Is it possible to get some fresh air and go for a walk in pleasant surroundings? (See chapters by Steve Epner and by Rose Jonas and Ellen Sweets in this volume.)

- **Announcement** – The invitation should come from (or have clear endorsement of) the organization's top leaders. The organization's board chair or director should highlight the importance of the retreat and signal enthusiasm and a clear commitment to acting on the results. The retreat planners should request RSVPs, and personally contact people whose participation they think will be especially important.

- **Agenda** – What outcomes do we want from the retreat? What's the schedule of work? Remember to build in plenty of breaks and good, healthy food. (Additional suggestions about the agenda will be included in the retreat process section below.)

- **Facilitation** – Who will facilitate the retreat? If the resources are available, the planners should consider hiring an outside facilitator who can act as a neutral "process guardian" and whose presence will allow everyone else to participate fully. (See Terrie Temkin's chapter in this volume.)

- **Materials, handouts, equipment** – What materials, handouts, and equipment are needed for conducting the retreat and any exercises? Make sure they are available.

- **Data gathering** – What information do we need to collect – including from stakeholders – so we are well prepared to do our work at the retreat? Distribute information in advance, if possible. (See Thomas Bakewell's chapter in this volume.)

RETREAT PROCESS

Atmosphere. Establishing an informal atmosphere is important at the outset in order to foster creativity and the intangible outcomes noted earlier. The challenge for retreat planners and facilitators will be to sustain informality while keeping the group more or less on schedule. Above all, they should be sure to provide adequate occasions for people to think and talk. In other words, conscious attention needs to be given to creating "free spaces" and "islands of imagination."

A good example of a retreat that provided such occasions was a visioning exercise held a few years ago at Santa Clara University in Santa Clara, CA. The organizers invited public, nonprofit and for-profit community leaders from the Silicon Valley, along with academic experts from the U.S. and Canada, to meet at the university's art museum to help craft a potential vision for the region. CEO's of Silicon Valley giants, prominent venture capitalists, and government, foundation, and nonprofit leaders were deeply concerned about the area's future viability. Issues tied to affordable housing, transportation networks, civic infrastructure, social capital and other topics threatened to diminish quality of life and choke off economic growth. The agenda included hour-long breaks during which participants were encouraged to form small groups, visit the art exhibits, and to stroll around campus or visit the chapel. The informal groups helped participants build relationships and understanding, find common ground, and lay the groundwork for the kind of concerted action that would be necessary to share the vision and enroll others in its realization.

Introduction. The agenda, including the purpose and desired outcomes, should be distributed. The facilitator may ask the board chair or executive director to welcome everyone. Participants should be allowed to ask questions about the purpose of the retreat, and helpful suggestions for modifying the agenda should be considered. Two options for an introductory exercise– the Hopes and Fears exercise, or a light-hearted icebreaker – are discussed below. The Hopes and Fears exercise may be best if the group is anxious about the retreat's outcomes. It allows participants to inspire each other with their best hopes for the retreat and admit (and at least partially dispel) the fears that they may have about – for example – whether the time spent will be worthwhile.

The Hopes and Fears Exercise can most easily be done with large Post-Its or half sheets of inexpensive letter-size paper and masking tape.

- Step 1. Ask participants to brainstorm on a sheet of paper their best hopes for the retreat.

- Step 2. Ask participants to star the most important three items.

- Step 3. Have them use a felt-tip marker to write each of the starred items in large letters on a large Post-It or half-sheet of paper. They should use only five to seven words.

- Step 4. Ask participants to stick their Post-Its on a wall, or else place a tape roll on the back of each half-sheet of paper and stick it on the wall. Like ideas should be placed together in columns or clusters.

- Step 5. Ask participants to decide whether the hopes are arranged in logical groups and rearrange any hopes that seem to be out of place.

- Step 6. Ask participants to name each column or cluster and place a Post-It or half-sheet of paper with the name at the top of the column. Be sure to use a differently colored marker or a border to highlight the name card.

- Step 7. Repeat steps 1-6 for fears that the participants have about the retreat process.

- Step 8. Prompt the group to talk about the results.

A possible light-hearted icebreaker begins with the facilitator's asking everyone to find a partner, or else assigning everyone a partner. Each partner then tells the other something intriguing about himself or herself that the group is unlikely to know; then the partners introduce each other to the larger group with a reference to the heretofore undisclosed information. The exercise disconnects people from their roles and highlights unexpected connections at a more human level. (Other ideas for icebreakers can be found in Carol Weisman's chapter in this volume.)

To help the group set ground rules for the retreat, the facilitator can build on the Hopes and Fears Exercise (or use other methods presented in Kristin Arnold's chapter in this volume). He or she could ask the group to identify ground rules that would help them realize the most compelling of the hopes and avoid the worst fears.

Stakeholder Analysis. Attention to the organization's key stakeholders is vital to developing effective mission and vision statements, since organizations basically exist in order to serve their stakeholders. Said differently, organizations that ignore this fact are doomed to failure. A stakeholder is "any person, group or organization that can place a claim on the organization's resources, attention, or output, or that is affected by its output" (Bryson and Alston, 1996, 43). A stakeholder analysis identifies the organization's internal and external stakeholders and considers "how they evaluate the organization, how they influence the organization, what the organization needs from them, and how important they are" (ibid.). The stakeholder analysis can be done as part of a mission and vision retreat, or prepared in advance.

The following three-step stakeholder analysis works best for groups of 12 or fewer participants. When conducting a retreat for more than a dozen people, split the group up into small groups of less than 10, ask each group to complete the exercises and then provide time for plenary sessions in which the groups report to each other.

- Step 1. Ask participants to brainstorm a list of key internal and external stakeholders and prepare a flipchart sheet that arrays them as illustrated in Figure 1.

- Step 2. For each stakeholder, prepare a stakeholder analysis worksheet (see Figure 2). In filling out the worksheets, be attentive to different perspectives and needs based on gender, ethnicity, physical ability, age, and religious preferences.

- Step 3. Discuss the implications of the stakeholder analysis for the organization's mission and vision.

More elaborate stakeholder analyses are possible and often desirable. See Bryson, Cunningham and Lokkesmoe (2002) for examples and references.

Mandates. An organization's mission and vision must take into account the formal and informal mandates imposed on the organization. These mandates might be contained in the organization's charter, in government laws or regulations, or in funders' stipulations. If the retreat is for a unit of a larger organization, the larger organization's mission is, in effect, a mandate for the unit.

One issue is how much attention to give to mandates. The planning team could simply list the mandates, bring them to the retreat and have the group list the requirements that stem from the mandates and clarify what is permitted (or not ruled out) by the mandates. However, it is also important to identify any mandates that are outmoded and to decide what to do about them.

Figure 1. Stakeholder Identification

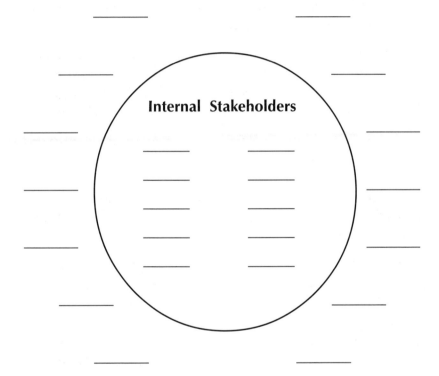

External Stakeholders

Internal Stakeholders

Source: Bryson, John M., and Farnum Alston. *Creating and Implementing Your Strategic Plan: A Workbook for Public and Nonprofit Organizations.* San Francisco: Jossey-Bass, 1996.

Figure 2. Stakeholder Analysis Worksheet

Stakeholder:			
Criteria Used by Stakeholders to Assess Our Performance	Our Sense of Their Judgment about Our Performance		
	Very Good	Okay	Poor

How do they influence us?

What do we need from them?

How important are they?

❑ Extremely

❑ Reasonably

❑ Not very

❑ Not at all

Source: Bryson, John M., and Farnum Alston. *Creating and Implementing Your Strategic Plan: A Workbook for Public and Nonprofit Organizations.* San Francisco: Jossey-Bass, 1996.

Thus, if an overall retreat purpose is to review an existing mission, participants should assess how well the mission and mandates align with each other and what changes might be needed in the mission to respond to the mandates. Alternatively, the group may develop ideas for changing the mandates so that the mission will be better served. If the retreat is creating a new mission, participants should consider how the mission will take the mandates into account. If the retreat is part of a full-blown strategic planning process, a complete analysis of the mandates should be done before developing the mission statement.

Organizational Highs and Lows. Clarifying what was involved in organizational successes and failures, or at least difficult times, can provide very useful insights into organizational history, viable strategies, and the nature of the mission itself.

- Preparation: Place six flipchart sheets on the wall (3 across and 2 down, overlapping at the edges). Draw a horizontal line across the midpoint of the flipcharts. At the left side of the line, write the year of the organization's founding and at the right, the current date. You may want to divide the line further into years or decades. Give participants 3x3 Post-It notes and black felt-tip markers.

- Step 1. Ask each participant to list on a sheet of paper all the major organizational successes that he or she can identify during the time period that appears on the wall. Everyone should star the top five and write each of these in large letters on a Post-It note. Be sure to include the year (or a more exact date) when the success occurred.

- Step 2. Invite the participants to place the Post-It notes on the flipchart sheets at the appropriate points along the time line and at a distance above the horizontal line that indicates the magnitude of success.

- Step 3. Ask each participant to list on a sheet of paper all the major organizational failures or difficulties that he or she can identify during the time period that appears on the wall. Everyone should star the top five and write each of these in large letters on a Post-It note. Be sure to include the year (or a more exact date) when the problem occurred.

- Step 4. Invite the participants to place the Post-It notes on the flipchart sheets at the appropriate points along the time line and at a distance below the horizontal line that indicates the magnitude of difficulty.

- Step 5. Invite participants to identify themes or patterns connected to the events above the line.

- Step 6. Invite participants to identify themes or patterns connected to the events below the line.

- Step 7. Have participants identify implications of these themes or patterns for the organization's mission.

Mission Elements. The group at the retreat should not try to develop or refine the actual mission statement. That task should be left to a single person or small group, as trying to wordsmith a mission statement in a large group is usually a frustrating misuse of people's time. Instead, the group at the retreat should provide all of the raw material needed to craft or refine a mission statement. If the group is developing a new mission statement, use the following procedure:

Ask participants to answer the following six questions silently as individuals, not as a group. Have them record their answers to each question on separate large Post-Its or half-sheets of paper, one answer per Post-It. Then aggregate individual answers by sticking them on a wall and clustering similar answers together. In other words, if an individual has several different answers to question one, he or she would use as many Post-Its as there were answers. If the person had six answers in total to the six questions, he or she would use six Post-Its all told. Alternatively, have people silently brainstorm answers to the questions on prepared worksheets, and then go around the room in round-robin fashion recording answers onto flipchart sheets.

The six questions are (Bryson, 1995, 75-78):

1. Who are we? What is our purpose? What business are we in?

2. In general, what are the basic social and political needs we exist to fill? Or what are the basic social or political problems we exist to address?

3. In general, what do we want to do to recognize or anticipate and respond to these needs or problems?

4. How should we respond to our key stakeholders?

5. What is our philosophy and what are our core values?

6. What makes us distinct or unique?

Once answers are recorded, either on clustered Post-Its on a wall or on flipchart sheets attached to a wall, give each participant eighteen sticky green dots and six sticky red dots (3/4 – 1 inch in diameter). Tell people they have three green dots and one red dot per question. For each question, ask everyone to place a green dot by the three answers that he or she deems most important for inclusion in the mission statement. Ask everyone to place a red dot by the one answer – if any – that he or she cannot abide.

If the group is reviewing an existing mission statement, you may not need to ask all of the above questions. It may be enough to hand out a copy of the existing mission and to ask the following:

1. Is our current mission dated, and if so how?

2. What changes in the mission do I propose?

Strategy Analysis. A mission is useless if it cannot be implemented. It therefore is important to test the existing or proposed mission against existing strategies (or in the case of a brand new organization, contemplated strategies). Use the following steps to assess the mission:

- Step 1. Ask participants to identify key organizational strategies and, especially, the consequences of each. Record answers in two columns – strategies and consequences – on flipchart sheets.

- Step 2. Based on these consequences, what does the organization's mission seem to be? Record answers on flipchart sheets.

- Step 3. How do the answers recorded in step 2 correspond to the final flipchart sheets prepared in the Mission Elements exercise? Write discrepancies on a flipchart sheet.

- Step 4. How do we respond to these discrepancies? Do we modify, subtract, or add elements to the mission statement, or do we change strategies?

If there is time, a group that is reviewing existing mission and vision statements might also do a time allocation exercise. In preparation the facilitator writes elements of the existing mission and vision on flipchart sheets and gives each participant 10 sticky dots, all the same color.

- Step 1. Explain that each dot represents 10 percent of each person's time on the job. Ask participants to allocate their dots among the mission and vision elements according to how they spend their time.

- Step 2. Give participants 10 sticky dots of another color and ask them to allocate these dots according to how they think they *should* be spending their time.

- Step 3. Ask participants how this exercise might prompt a change to the mission and vision statements.

Vision Collage. In preparation for this exercise, ask participants to bring to the retreat photographs, symbols, or other materials that they think may be useful in developing a vision of what the organization might look like as it successfully implements its strategies and fulfills its potential. Begin by dividing the group into small groups of six or less. Give each a flipchart sheet, colored markers, scissors, colored paper, stickers, glue sticks and any other materials that might be useful in fostering creativity. Invite them to use the photos and other materials they have brought. You may want to play a peaceful CD in the background. Give the groups 45 minutes to an hour to develop a striking collage that communicates their ideas of what the organization might be at its best. Advise them to rely as little as possible on words. (Indeed, this exercise can be especially effective with groups that do not have high-level writing skills.)

Once the collages are complete, have the groups put them on the wall and invite the people who were not among the creators to comment on the messages they see in each collage. Then ask the creators to comment. Be sure someone is recording the most insightful responses. Finally, record the main messages on a flipchart sheet and discuss them as a whole. The committee assigned to draft an organizational vision statement will use this flipchart sheet as a key resource.

Action Steps. The final part of the retreat should be devoted to selecting a committee that will draft the mission and vision statements and to outlining a plan for reviewing, adopting, and implementing the statements. The facilitator may simply ask for volunteers for the committee, but also should probably allow participants to nominate others who they feel are especially gifted in crafting compelling messages. The group also should agree on a reasonable timeline for producing a draft and a plan for circulating it throughout the organization and responding to comments. In deciding on next steps, the following questions should be considered:

1. What official bodies – for example, the board of directors – will need to approve the statements? What do we need to do to place the statements on their agendas?

2. What actions must we take to ensure that the mission and vision statements are prominent in organizational publications, mailings, the website, our offices, and the events we sponsor, as well as in our ongoing deliberations, recruitment, and staff development efforts?

3. What is our plan for periodically reviewing the mission and vision statements?

4. What kind of celebration might we plan to highlight the significance of adopting the mission and vision statements?

5. Who will be responsible for the various tasks we have identified in this part of the retreat?

Closing. Take a few minutes at the very end of the retreat to recognize each other for your hard work. and celebrate your accomplishments. You may want to encourage each participant to say a few words about what was most meaningful about the retreat. You should save the flipchart sheets and collages to document the group's work and provide guidance for the drafting committee.

Tying Up Loose Ends. At a successful retreat an enormous amount of good will and work will have been expended, and a great deal of important material will have been developed and discussed. It is important not to lose any of the materials or to squander any of the good will and good work. Make sure that all materials are collected, make sure the "To Do" lists are formulated, and make sure that the groups responsible for next steps meet briefly to confirm times, dates, and responsibilities for their next meeting.

Conclusion

As noted in the introduction, it is easy to justify spending organizational resources on a retreat to produce something as important to an organization's success as compelling, inspiring mission and vision statements. A well-designed retreat for this purpose can enhance organizational articulation of, and commitment to, the high calling that the organization is meant to embody and serve. Organizational members, other key stakeholders, and society as a whole should be better off. If a retreat is to foster such outcomes, it must create what Evans and Boyte (1986) call a "free space," or what we call an "island of the imagination." These are spaces in which a group of people can summon and give voice to the soul and spirit of their organization. Careful attention to preparation, agenda design, facilitation, and follow-up can create the occasions and results that clarify an organization's soul, spirit, and reason for being – and how the world will be better for it.

References

Angelica, Emil. *Crafting Effective Mission and Vision Statements.* St. Paul, MN: Amherst H. Wilder Foundation, 2001.

Bryson, John M. *Strategic Planning for Public and Nonprofit Organizations.* San Francisco: Jossey-Bass, 1995.

Bryson, John M., and Farnum Alston. *Creating and Implementing Your Strategic Plan: A Workbook for Public and Nonprofit Organizations.* San Francisco: Jossey-Bass, 1996.

Bryson, John M, and Sharon Anderson. "Applying Large-Group Interaction Methods in the Planning and Implementation of Major Change Efforts." *Public Administration Review*, 60 (2), 2000, 143-162.

Bryson, John M., Gary Cunningham and Karen Lokkesmoe. "What To Do When Stakeholders Matter: The Case of Problem Formulation for the African American Men Project of Hennepin County, Minnesota," *Public Administration Review*, 62 (5), 2002, 568-584.

Evans, Sara, and Harry Boyte. *Free Spaces.* Philadelphia: Temple University Press, 1986.

Friend, John and Allen Hickling. *Planning Under Pressure.* Oxford, England: Butterworth-Heinemann, 1997.

Holm, Bill. *Eccentric Islands.* Minneapolis: Milkweed Press, 2001.

Holman, Peggy and Tom Devane. *The Change Handbook.* San Francisco: Berrett-Koehler, 1999.

John M. Bryson, Ph.D.

I knew I wanted to meet John Bryson when I was taking a graduate course in strategic planning for nonprofits. His book *Strategic Planning for Public and Nonprofit Organizations* was the clearest, most useful, best-written text book I had ever used. It is also the only one that nine years later, I frequently refer to.

John Bryson grew up in State College, Pennsylvania, home of Penn States. He was more shocked by Penn State joining the Big Ten than the collapse of the Soviet Union. With perseverance and strength, he has recovered from both.

John went to Cornell University as an undergraduate where he studied economics and student activism. The good news is that he was never formally arrested. It doesn't really matter now if there is a tap on his phones. When his two college age kids are home, he can't get a turn to use it anyway. John has always had creative solutions to everything. He missed being sent to Vietnam by being a member of the US White Water Canoeing and Kayaking Team and then became a Vista Volunteer in Georgia.

John did all of his graduate work at the University of Wisconsin where he studied urban and regional planning. The weather was cooler, and the police heat was off. However, during the tumultuous time in the seventies, he was gassed out of his apartment once. John went to the Hubert Humphrey Institute of Public Affairs at the University of Minnesota and has been there ever since.

John met his wife, colleague and co-author Barbara in Georgia. She was a reporter for the *Augusta Herald*. He was on her beat. They met for coffee every Thursday morning to consult on stories and one thing led to another.

In 2002-2003 they are doing a sabbatical year at the University of Strathclyde in Scotland where John will be rewriting my favorite textbook.

Prof. John M. Bryson
Humphrey Institute of Public Affairs
University of Minnesota
301 19th Avenue S., Minneapolis, MN 55455
612-625-5888
E-mail: HYPERLINK "mailto:jmbryson@hhh.umn.edu"
jmbryson@hhh.umn.edu

Barbara C. Crosby, Ph.D.

Barbara Crosby has spent the last two decades puzzling about the meaning of leadership, teaching courses and consulting, and handling the usual challenges of midlife. She's still not sure she's got leadership completely pinned down, but she has written two books on the topic (*Leadership for the Common Good,* published by Jossey-Bass and *Leadership for Global Citizenship*, published by Sage).

Before teaching and writing about leadership, Barbara was a newspaper reporter and editor, and then press secretary and speechwriter for governors of Wisconsin and Minnesota. As the granddaughter of South Carolina sharecroppers, she got a special kick out of writing speeches for Minnesota governor Rudy Perpich, the son of immigrants from the former Yugoslavia.

Barbara grew up in Augusta, Georgia, graduated from Vanderbilt University, and worked as a journalist in Augusta and Baltimore, before migrating to the frozen north in the mid 1970s to attend graduate school, not coincidentally at the same place (University of Wisconsin) where John Bryson was studying.

Despite Barbara's vows not to move further north, she and John, now married, relocated to Minneapolis in 1977 and have lived there ever since, except for sabbatical years in England and Scotland. Barbara joined the Reflective Leadership Center at the Humphrey Institute of Public Affairs, University of Minnesota, in 1982 and has remained fascinated by the interplay of leadership and public policy ever since. Though she made another vow, once completing her master's degree, never to return to graduate school, she found the subject of leadership so seductive that in the mid-1990s she obtained her Ph.D. in leadership studies from the Union Institute.

Fortunately, her children and spouse were still speaking to her when she was done with her doctorate. And, by the way, Barbara does keep vows other than those having to do with degrees and where to live.

Barbara C. Crosby, Ph.D.
Humphrey Institute of Public Affairs
301 19th Avenue S., Minneapolis, MN 55455
E-mail: bcrosby@hhh.umn.edu.

CHAPTER 8

Establishing
Organizational Values

Alan D. Goodman, MSW, CSW

I dentifying and clearly articulating the underlying values of nonprofit organizations are critical steps in any planning and visioning process. Doing so provides a firm foundation upon which an organization can establish effective organizational policies procedures and practices.

This chapter provides a context for understanding the relationship between organizational values, policies and practices. It also explains why it is important for an organization to identify and articulate its values. It offers a practical "how to" guide containing a suggested format, process and tools to help steer your organization through a values clarification process. Finally, it provides case studies as well as an easily adaptable organizational values checklist and worksheet.

A Conceptual Framework for
Personal and Organizational Values

DEFINITION OF "VALUES"

The Webster's University Dictionary defines a value as a "principle, standard or quality regarded as worthwhile or desirable." [1] What follows is an exploration of this concept as it ultimately applies to nonprofit organizations.

---

[1] Webster's II New Riverside University Dictionary, The Riverside Publishing Company, 1988.

Individual Values

- *Can be conscious or unconscious.*
- *Are adopted through socialization, culture and experience.*
- *Are "coded into our brains," cannot be easily seen and are rarely questioned.*
- *Carry emotional charges.*
- *Are subjective and do not need to be proved.*
- *Are action oriented.*
- *Provide a framework for individuals to make choices based upon their beliefs.*
- *Are directly connected to ethical conduct.*
- *Are aggregated into community values (and further reflected in government policy).*

As individuals, we hold specific values, consciously or unconsciously, that are shaped (in part) by our cultural environments. These values have been passed to us through a socialization process by our parents, our school systems, our religious leaders and teachers, and our communities. Our life experiences and the environment within which we live (including our contact with popular media) also influence our values.

Values carry emotional charges. This means that there is a direct connection between our values and our feelings. We may feel more intense about some values than others (Linzer 1996). "People make greater personal investments in values that are felt more deeply and are more abiding. This is because values tend to be inculcated during childhood and represent parents' dreams and ideals for their children." [2]

---

[2] Norman Linzer, "Ethical Dilemmas in Jewish Communal Service" 1996 KTAV pg. 3

Charlotte Roberts[3] defines personal values as part of a mental model, which is composed of "deeply held views of what we find worthwhile." She distinguishes between "espoused values," which we profess to believe in, and our "values in action," which are supposed to correlate directly with our espoused values, but actually direct our behavior. Values in action operate on a primary, organic level, are "coded into our brains," cannot be easily seen and are rarely questioned. It is these qualities of "values in action" that create dissonance for us, because we rarely take the time to determine whether there is synergy between what we say we believe in and how we act.

Surprisingly, in a society that demands empirical proof or justification for statements of fact, value statements are not required to meet such rigorous standards. Values need not be testable, are unashamedly subjective in nature and can be asserted without the need to defend or prove them (Levy 1979, cited in Linzer). [4]

Values are action-oriented and lead the individual to make choices and act based upon his or her value system and beliefs. John Carver (1990) identifies the direct link between the values that we hold, our perception of reality and our behavior. "As individuals, our behavior grows out of our perspectives and values as we confront external realities. Under a certain condition, our values and perspectives lead us to act in a certain manner. We are valuing, conceptualizing beings, who constantly seek to make sense out of our world and ourselves, by linking sense data with frameworks. The sense data are our more or less reliable measures of 'reality'; the frameworks are our values and perspectives." [5]

There is, therefore, a direct connection between our own unique values and the action that we choose to take because of them. Once we have identified and understood what those values are, we can de-

---

3   Charlotte Roberts, "Checklist for Personal Values," in Peter Senge, "The Fifth Discipline Fieldbook," Doubleday, New York, 1994, pg. 209

4   Linzer pg.4

5   John Carver, "Boards That Make a Difference: A New Design for Leadership in Nonprofit and Public Organizations," Jossey Bass, San Francisco, 1990, pg. 26

termine what our behavior should be as we encounter specific situations. It is this "ought" component in values that makes the connection between values and ethical conduct (Levy 1979, cited in Linzer).[6]

Organizational Values

- *Are building blocks that sustain organizations and keep them healthy.*

- *Exert a powerful and often invisible influence on organizations.*

- *Are created, maintained and sustained through the will and effort of individuals.*

- *Are enduring.*

- *Are directly linked to the organization's mission, vision, principles, philosophies and priorities.*

- *Are communicated through board policies.*

- *Determine organizational circumstances, activities and goals.*

- *Are actualized through the programs and services provided by the organization.*

Peter Drucker reinforces the importance of positive outcomes for organizations, but also views organizational values as indispensable building blocks that sustain organizations and keep them vibrant and healthy. "Direct results always come first. In the care and feeding of an organization, they play the role calories play in the care and feeding of the human body. But any organization also needs a commitment to human values and their constant reaffirmation, as a human body needs vitamins and minerals. There has to be something this organization stands for, or else it degenerates into disorganization, confusion and paralysis."[7]

---

[6] Linzer, pg. 4

[7] Peter F. Drucker, "The Effective Executive," Harper Business, New York, 1993, pg. 56

Organizations are created, maintained and sustained through the will and effort of individuals. "Organizations are similar to individuals in these respects. Their frameworks of values and perspectives determine specific decisions and behaviors in the face of specific facts. And their choices of what to regard as relevant facts about the environment are themselves determined by the same frameworks. Values and perspectives are thus powerful, often invisible forces that determine not only organizational circumstances, activities and goals, but even the data that organizations admit into their assessment of reality." [8]

For example, in response to a high rate of teen pregnancy in a community, one organization may decide that the solution is to provide family planning services, educating teens about safe sex and distributing free contraceptives. Another organization, when reviewing the same data, may decide to approach the problem by offering programs to build self-esteem and educating teens about the benefits of abstinence before marriage. Both approaches may be equally effective in reducing the level of teen pregnancy.

These choices were undoubtedly directly related to each organization's underlying organizational value system. In the example above, the former may be reflective of an organization with "pro-choice" values and the latter with "pro-life" values. This value system itself would have been molded and strongly influenced by the enduring values of the organization's founders and current leadership.

"An organization's culture can be seen as its members' collective mental models – which is why you cannot change an organization without investigating its cultural assumptions." [9]

This influence can be clearly seen in faith-based organizations, where the tenets of the specific faith are incorporated into the organizations' culture and value systems and have a direct bearing on practice and services. The organizations' founders established the organizations in order to provide service to the community within

---

[8] Carver, pg.27

[9] Edgar H. Schein, "Organizational Culture and Leadership" (1985, 1992), San Francisco: Jossey Bass, in Senge pg. 267

the context of their own values and belief systems. It is not surprising therefore that an organization under Catholic auspices would not offer family planning or abortion services. A Jewish social service agency may be expected to offer programs and services that are designed to strengthen Jewish identity.

THE IMPORTANCE OF IDENTIFYING AND ARTICULATING ORGANIZATIONAL VALUES

It is important that the board identify organizational values in collaboration with key stakeholders and then clarify and communicate those values to the staff at all levels. "Nonprofits, perhaps more than most kinds of organizations, because they are value based organizations, must be anchored by a set of values which are shared by the staff and board. These values and the organization culture will be unconsciously and covertly developed and directed by the staff, unless the organization's board and staff seeks to clarify and define their shared values." [10] A suggested method for identifying organizational values is included below.

It is also important to understand that organizational values must provide the foundation upon which the organization's vision, mission, principles and priorities are based. For example, organizational values play an important part in defining what the organization will become involved in and must tie in directly with its mission. This is where "espoused values" and "values in action" come together; it is where the proverbial "rubber meets the road." Following is a brief definition of each of these concepts.

> *Vision:* An organization's values and its vision (a compelling, conceptual image of the future that the organization wishes to create) are directly linked to each other. This is because values describe in tangible terms how the organization intends to conduct its business in pursuit

[10] Jerry Cronin, "Organizational Mission and Values," pg. 31 in "The Nonprofit Board Book: Strategies for Organizational Success," Revised Edition, Eds. Earl Anthes, Jerry Cronin and Michael Jackson. West Memphis and Hampton, Arkansas Independent Community Consultants, 1985

of its future vision. The vision, therefore, embodies the organization's values within a future time frame in ways that can motivate and focus organizational activities.

Mission: The mission describes the purposes for which the organization was established. These purposes are invariably connected to the value systems of the founders who envisioned an organization that would embody their own values.

Principles: The core values and philosophies that describe how an organization conducts itself in carrying out its mission.

Priorities: The organizational priorities identify the most important areas that will be the focus of the finite resources available to the organization. Progress in accomplishing these priorities can be identified in terms of desired outcomes that are measurable. There is a direct correlation between these priorities and the organization's values. In effect, the priorities are the actualization of the values espoused by the organization.

Helping organizations consider either re-affirming or re-stating values a critical part of any planning or evaluation process. "Developing a vision and values is a messy, artistic process. Living it convincingly is a passionate one." (Peters 1991) [11]

THE INTERPLAY BETWEEN ORGANIZATIONAL VALUES AND THE COMMUNITY

Given the unique relationship between nonprofit organizations and the communities they serve, the synergy between organizational values and those of the community is critical. The community needs to implicitly trust that the organization is honoring the community's values and that the organization's integrity is beyond reproach. The

---

[11] Tom Peters, "Thriving on Chaos: Handbook for A Management Revolution," Alfred A Knopf, New York, 1991, pg. 401

organization is, therefore, accountable to the community and must be able to demonstrate that its actions reflect the community's values. Moreover, the organization is obliged to clearly, accurately and effectively communicate its values, policies and procedures to the public. Communication can occur through solicitation and public relations materials, public service announcements, and written audits, policies and other documents that reflect the organization's "values in action."

"It might be argued that relatively open discussion of philosophy and values actually might damage an organization's effectiveness. Because only publicly acceptable philosophies and values are likely to be discussed in public, an organization whose success depends on pursuit of publicly unacceptable values could suffer. Public discussion of the agency's philosophy and values therefore might require the organization to change its strategy and, as a result, become less effective." [12]

COMMUNICATING ORGANIZATIONAL VALUES THROUGH POLICY

In most nonprofit organizations, staff members provide direct services to consumers and interact daily with the public. It is, therefore, staff interpretation of the values that will influence the manner in which the values are put into practice. There could be a substantial difference between the values as espoused and the values as manifested through action. In order to ensure the implementation of espoused organizational values, and for legal and business reasons, policies must be established to guide the staff in its work.

Organizations need to constantly make value choices when conducting their affairs. These choices have a major impact on the organizations' very nature and destinies. The results of these value choices are very often contained within the documentation

---

[12] John M. Bryson, "Strategic Planning for Public and Nonprofit Organizations: A guide to Strengthening and Sustaining Organizational Achievement," Jossey Bass Publishers, San Francisco, 1988, pg. 109

that is generated by each organization, be it programmatic (program policies, descriptions, eligibility requirements), fiscal (budgets, payment methods, insurance coverage for employees) or related to resource development (solicitation materials, donor correspondence, Web site messages).

The underlying question relates to how these decisions are made. Has the staff made these choices by default or has the board provided guidance through policy determination or other means? Boards have a central role in this arena and need to have an unwavering focus on "what we are here for" to make sure that they are providing the values framework within which the organization functions. Without this focus, staff members must make many of these value decisions alone, or they must be settled by default. (Carver, 1990) [13]

One of the primary roles of the board therefore is to identify, clarify and communicate the value system by developing explicit policies that the staff brings to life through organizational activities. "Values dominate policies that are instructive to staff, that is, policies that tell staff what to do or not to do. So whether a board wishes narrowly to control or more expansively to lead, governing through policies is the efficient way to operate." [14]

Therefore, an important factor to consider when recruiting board members is the prospective member's comfort level and competency in that aspect of policy development that relates to values clarification, organizational vision and the long-term significance of these endeavors for organizational integrity and vitality. "Those members who make the best contributions are those who have a natural propensity to look not only beyond the stream of single events, but beyond systems to the values upon which they are based. It is only a small step from divining today's values as they are, to planning tomorrow's values as they should be." [15]

---

[13] Carver pg. 71

[14] Carver pg. 28

[15] Carver pg. 202

Putting Organizational Policies
that Reflect Values into Action

During the incorporation process, nonprofit organizations formally identify their mission. They then become legally accountable to the community (consumers, board, staff, members of the public, state and federal government) for acting in a manner compatible with their stated missions. By definition, they are also accountable for upholding the underlying values upon which these missions are based.

To illustrate this point, an organization that states that it has been established specifically to provide advocacy and support services to the working poor, but does not have evening or weekend hours of operation and cannot be reached by public transportation, would not be acting in a manner that is compatible with its stated mission. This would represent a clear conflict between the organization's espoused values and its values as manifested through action.

This same principle would apply with regard to espoused values as they relate to internal organizational issues. "If your organization believes that 'employees are our most important asset,' it means that your first strategy in difficult times will not be layoffs. You may eventually have to lay off people, but it will be carefully considered, because it contradicts your organization's (espoused) value in action." [16]

So simply articulating values that ' have always been reflective of who we are,' or those that the organization thinks the community will respond well to or expects to hear, will serve neither the organization nor the community's best interests unless they are acted upon. "Clarity about philosophy and core values will help an organization maintain its integrity." [17]

Articulating a set of values to which neither the board nor staff ascribe will make it impossible for these values to be upheld or reflected in everyday decision-making and action. This could also lead to the organization misreading the challenges and opportunities that

---

[16] Charlotte Roberts in Senge pg. 209

[17] Bryson pg. 53

it encounters in its environment. Organizations that do not pay attention to the organizational philosophies and core values are likely to misread their strengths and weaknesses. Consequently, they may choose strategies that are doomed to failure because they are not consistent with these philosophies and values. [18]

Similarly, espousing values through the implementation of policies that are (or appear to be) at variance with those of the community the organization operates within can have a major effect on public trust.

An Organization's Values Evolve

An organization's mission and values are amenable to change as leadership and community needs evolve. A change in core values and mission may enable organizations to more accurately reflect community values and more effectively meet community needs. As organizations evolve and values and perspectives are modified or change appreciably, the "value history" can be traced through the explicit policies that have been produced and documented by the board. "This type of documentation provides a sense of history and tradition, without perforce binding anyone to the traditional." [19]

The following case study, illustrating the experience of a family-service-based adoption program, dramatically demonstrates the key role that staff decisions can have on organizational policy implementation and ultimately, the impact on consumers. It shows the enormous impact that individual values can have on organizational policy.

A Case Study: Adoption Policy Implementation and It's impact on Adoptive Parents, Birth Parents and Adoptees in The Family Service Agency

Family service agencies across the country have traditionally played a role in adoption services, making adoption a viable option for childless couples of modest means. Programs in some organizations have waned and often been eliminated

---

[18] Bryson pg. 99

[19] Carver pg. 190

because of difficulties in finding healthy newborn babies available for adoption. Competition with specialized adoption agencies, attorneys and physicians involved in adoptions has further eroded the availability of infants. In order to maintain their programs in response to the substantial demand by individuals and couples for healthy infants, traditional family service agencies have had to develop new strategies. Such strategies have included "open adoptions" (where the birth mother chooses the adoptive family and sometimes remains involved with the child's new family), international adoptions and post-adoption services for entities without the trained staff and licensing to provide these services.

These agencies retain adoption case records that must be created, maintained and either secured or made available based upon state law. In concert with the changes that occurred in The Family Service Agency's adoption program strategies (and in compliance with state law), the agency's board of trustees established policy to give birth parents the choice to make future contact with the children they released upon a child's reaching adulthood. To implement this policy, the staff developed a declaration form, upon which the birth parents could indicate whether they wished to have future contact with the baby they released for adoption. In this way, when an adult adoptee requested contact with a birth parent, the agency staff would refer to the form and, if the birth parent had indicated so, would contact the birth parent. If the form indicated "no contact," the agency staff would not make contact and would not provide the adult adoptee with information. Signed declaration forms were retained in the adoption case file.

During interviews with the senior adoption worker as part of creating a records retention policy, the worker explained to the records management consultant that the adoption case files almost always contained forms stating that birth parents were not interested in contact with their offspring. All signed forms said "no contact" because agency staff members were instructed to strongly advise all birth parents to indicate that they were not interested in future contact. They told birth parents that they could always change their minds (and the form) later.

The rationale given by the senior worker was that because this was an extremely emotional time for typically very young birth parents, signing "no contact" was a more cautious decision. She advised further that when they were more mature and less emotional, they could reverse the decision and change the declaration. As most birthparents would not remember that they had signed such a declaration (amid the myriad papers they signed at a very emotional time many years earlier), the record stating that they did not want to have contact would effectively preclude this from happening, especially as there would have been staff turnover by the time the child reached adulthood.

The worker's personal views about "adoption reunion" decision-making clearly had a major impact on agency policy implementation. In this case, the impact was the opposite of what the board had intended.

Secrets of a Successful Retreat to Help Organizations Identify Core Values

A discussion of organizational values requires time, energy and effort. Sufficient time must be set aside to thoroughly explore this issue and to incorporate what is learned. A half-day retreat, with light refreshments should be sufficient, provided that preparatory work has been done in advance and follow-up actions are taken afterward.

USING AN OUTSIDE FACILITATOR

The process of identifying and adopting organizational values could produce substantial disagreement, particularly if the participants represent diverse backgrounds. The use of an outside facilitator is strongly recommended.

A facilitator can help the organization explore areas of disagreement rather than conceal them and also ensure a "safe" environment, where a productive and open discussion can be held. The facilitator helps to create a level playing field, where every participant is equal. Staff, management, board members, consumers and community representatives all join the activity as full participants. Each participant can be held to the same standards as everyone else and can learn to understand and appreciate other points of view. Because the desired outcomes of this process will be clear, the facilitator can be held accountable for helping groups reach this point by the conclusion of the retreat.

A. Before The Retreat:
Preparatory Work Required

Using a structured format and specific tools to guide the discussion will greatly enhance the experience for participants and ensure a positive outcome. It is also important to be as inclusive as possible in order to promote extensive "buy in" by all interested parties. This requires that information be gathered from individuals who will not be participating in the retreat itself. Planning for the retreat should include these and other issues that will be enumerated below. Following are tips and tools related to these actions.

Identify the Need and Enumerate the Potential Benefits for the Organization

Taking this first step is essential, to smooth the way for the steps that follow and to ensure a positive outcome.

Establish Board and Staff Champions

Because this concept will need to be "sold" to the board and senior staff members, it is important to establish champions in both of these groups. It will be their role and reputation in the organization that will help to make other members of the board and staff take notice and carefully consider this recommendation. Once they understand and endorse the importance of the values clarification process, they, too, can begin to advocate for this to be done. Ideally, the president (chairman of the board) and the executive director (ED) or chief professional officer (CPO) should fully support this idea.

Present the Proposal to the Board and Get Board Approval

The purpose of this is threefold. First, the policy- making role of the board makes it essential that the board members understand not only what the values are, but how they are related to policy-making. Second, strong board participation in the retreat is desirable, in order for the outcomes to be credible. Finally, having board approval to do this will increase the likelihood that the results of this process will be used for the benefit of the organization.

The board will need to understand why this is being done, the expected outcomes, the benefit for the organization, the process, the time commitment and the costs.

Here is an example of how this could be presented:

Sample Materials for Board Presentation

Our **purpose** is to identify and reach consensus on the underlying core values upon which our organization is built.

The expected **outcomes** will be: consensus on a clearly defined list of core values for our organization. A written report that makes specific recommendations on the next steps to be taken. *See examples of organizational values from other organizations.*

The **benefit to our organization** will be that we can use these values to redefine our mission statement, create a clear vision of our organization's future and identify organizational policies to guide and focus our work. This will help to make us more effective, enable us to make sound business decisions when faced with challenges and opportunities and will help us to remain viable and strong.

The **process** will include: establishing a planning committee, comprised of board, staff and other key

continued

---

individuals; conducting a half-day retreat; gathering information prior to the retreat and presenting a final report and recommendations to the board

The **time commitment** will be for a half-day retreat. This is an important priority and we expect all board members to participate, either in the retreat or in other information sharing. For those who are invited to participate on the planning committee, there will be an additional time commitment.

The **costs** associated with this process should be estimated in case board approval is required. A "not to exceed" figure can be established which will enable the planning committee to do its work effectively.

Involve Stakeholders and Invite them to Participate

Stakeholders are any individuals that identify with or have an investment in the organization, its mission and/or its programs and services. This includes board, staff, consumers, funders and other interested parties. Since not all of these individuals can be included in the retreat itself, other means of ensuring their participation in the process must be identified. The overall rules of thumb are to be as inclusive as possible, to clarify why the stakeholders input is valuable and to communicate how this input will be used.

Define the Overall Process

Participants will be more willing and able to participate effectively if they understand the process. For example, a process similar to the following may be defined and communicated:

In order to accomplish our goals, we will:

- **Establish a planning group.**
  After board approval, the planning group should be established. The composition of this group should be

determined by the president and the ED, and should be composed of board, staff members and other stakeholders. The group should be no larger than five to seven individuals and should be authorized to proceed without requiring further board approval.

- **Identify the chairperson (lay) for the planning group and the retreat.**
  A key member of the board, other than the board president, should be appointed to this position. Ideally, this individual should be one of the "champions" identified earlier and should be chosen by the president and the ED.

- **Conduct a planning meeting prior to the retreat.**
  The goal of the meeting should be to identify all the issues that require attention and to plan and implement the process. An example of the issues to be discussed by the committee could be:

Sample Issues for the Policy Committee

1. Will an outside facilitator be used? What will be his or her involvement in the planning process?

2. Who will be invited to participate? *While inclusiveness and representation of all stakeholders are desirable, there should be no more than 20-25 participants for the retreat to be effective.*

3. How and when will the input of other stakeholders be solicited? *Because the number of participants at the retreat will be limited, other vehicles must be used to elicit their input (questionnaires, focus groups, interviews). See Organizational Values Checklist that can be adapted for any of these approaches.*

continued

---

4. How will this input be quantified and incorporated in the process? *Explain the process so that all participants understand how their feedback will be incorporated.*

5. What preparatory work will need to be done prior to the retreat and how, by whom and when will this be accomplished? *(Location; time needed; setup and equipment; refreshments).*

6. How will the retreat itself be structured? **See sample Program Process Outline.**

7. How and by whom will the final outcomes and recommendations be prepared and communicated? Who will they be communicated to? Will additional feedback be solicited from these individuals?

8. Will the anticipated costs for the exercise be kept within the approved budget parameters?

• **Collect Data from Stakeholders Not Participating in the Retreat**
  Analyze the data and determine the top five to 10 organizational values for each clearly defined group. *See Organizational Values Checklist and Worksheet*

B. DURING THE RETREAT: THE VALUES CLARIFICATION PROCESS.

This can be approached in many ways. If working with an outside facilitator, a customized approach should be developed with input from members of the planning committee. An example of a process that could be used is:

Sample Retreat Program Process Outline

- Divide participants into small discussion groups to get people thinking about values. Encourage participants to identify what they think the **original values** of the organization were when it was founded and their source. How are they manifested in action through the organization's services / programs? Provide a definition of "values" and identify key questions to guide the discussion.

  Note: *The purpose is to engage participants in the discussion and create an awareness and comfort level with the concepts. There are no right or wrong answers.*

- Report results of each group discussion. *Focus on the experience and not on content.*

- Define entire group perceptions of **what the organizational values should be.** Have each participant identify his or her own top 10 organizational values using the organizational values checklist (*see page 169*). Using the consensus model (*on following page*) identify the group's top 10 values and paste them up.

- Paste up the top 10 values of other clearly defined groups gathered prior to the retreat and discuss differences and similarities among them and the values identified during the retreat. Encourage participants to try and explain why these differences exist.

- Identify the top 10 (or more) common values from all lists combined. Using the consensus model, identify the group's top five values and paste them up.

- Discuss and help the group to loosely define what is meant by each of the top five values and to develop a preamble to the values. *See Sample Materials on the following pages.*

  Note: *Capture the central ideas, descriptive words and phrases only. Descriptions can be reworked after the retreat.*

C. AFTER THE RETREAT

- Write up the results and prepare recommendations for next steps.

- Send materials to retreat participants for feedback.

- Incorporate changes and finalize report.

- Communicate results to all participants and the community (Web site; newsletter, newspaper article, etc.) with thanks to those who participated in the process.

*   *   *   *   *

SAMPLE MATERIALS

The Consensus Model

Use this model to pare down and prioritize a list of items and to achieve group consensus.

1. Write up the list of items and paste it up, so everyone can see it. Make the list as inclusive as possible so everyone feels that his or her important items are listed.

2. Ask each participant to write down his or her top ten items from the list on a sheet of paper. This **need not be in priority order**.

3. Collect the lists and mark the number of votes each item receives on the master list, so everyone can see the results. Identify the top 10 items by number of votes received.

4. Ask each participant to rank the top 10 items **in order of priority** for themselves and to write them down.

5. Identify the top five items in priority order, based on the votes of participants.

SAMPLE ORGANIZATIONAL VALUES
The City of Harrisonburg, Virginia

The prosperity, harmony and livability of a community is a direct result of the interaction, trust and teamwork between its citizens, elected officials and employees. In striving to maintain our community as **"The City With The Planned Future,"** we pledge a commitment to the following *Organizational Values.*

WE VALUE AN OPEN AND ACCESSIBLE GOVERNMENT: In a democracy, a government must be a partnership between the citizens, elected officials and employees. We pledge to provide an open, honest government for our citizens that encourages their input and fosters a free exchange of ideas.

WE VALUE QUALITY SERVICE TO OUR CITIZENS: The city exists to provide services to its citizens. We pledge a commitment to enhance the value and quality of city services in terms of cost and performance.

WE VALUE FISCAL RESPONSIBILITY: Careful management of our financial resources demonstrates our respect for the citizens who provide the financial support for our organization. We pledge a commitment to the concept that fiscal responsibility recognizes that most problems cannot be solved by money alone, and thus demands fresh approaches and creativity in addressing issues in a cost-effective way.

WE VALUE A HUMANE ORGANIZATION: Work should be a source of enjoyment and satisfaction. We pledge to place great emphasis upon the personal qualities that contribute to a humane organization and foster a caring attitude.

WE VALUE EQUALITY IN OPPORTUNITY AND TREATMENT: Fair treatment and the opportunity to prosper are basic human needs that should be afforded to both employees and citizens. We pledge to treat people fairly and with understanding so that individuals are made to feel part of the community's team.

WE VALUE A SPIRIT OF PROFESSIONALISM: Successful completion of the task is more important than who gets the credit. We pledge to display a professional attitude that dictates a dispassionate analysis of issues, free of personal biases and with a commitment to the organization.

WE VALUE THE FUTURE: So many times the future is ignored in day-to-day operations and decision-making. We pledge to prepare for the future on a daily basis, ever mindful of the changing dynamics within our organization and the community and the need to have a long-term plan and strategy for dealing with these changing dynamics.

http://www.ci.harrisonburg.va.us/organ.html

CORE VALUES
Jewish Family Service Of Metropolitan Detroit

Preamble

The mission of the Jewish Family Service results in our being deeply involved in significant personal and professional issues in the lives of the individuals and families we serve. Our work creates unique challenges as we work with our community, to seek solutions to complex problems through our decision-making. The following core values are presented as a set of abiding beliefs to guide us in this process. The intent and spirit is to identify essential and enduring tenets that stand the test of time and offer guidance and reassurance.

Our Foundation

- An inherent obligation within Judaism is to help one another. While our primary focus is on the Jewish Community, we recognize a broader responsibility and openness to the general community.

Our Ethical Standards

- We behave in a manner consistent with Jewish values and ethical professional standards and with the highest degree of honesty and integrity.

Our Focus

- Our professional responsibility is first to serve our clients. We care about our clients; we care about our staff; we care about our community.

Our Approach

- We value independence and autonomy while promoting growth and development. We foster cooperation and collaboration, internally and externally. We strive for excellence in quality service and reach out in progressive and innovative ways to meet community needs.

The Reality

- As a not-for-profit organization, we are cognizant of our need to be fiscally responsible and to use our resources prudently.

Adapted and printed with permission the Jewish Family Service of Metropolitan Detroit.

ORGANIZATIONAL VALUES
Lewisville Police Department –
Community Policing

Partnership

We are committed to working in partnership with the community and each other to identify and resolve problems and issues that impact the safety of the citizens of our City.

Respect

We are committed to respecting individual rights, human dignity and the value of all members of the community and the Department.

Integrity

We are committed to nurturing the public trust by holding ourselves accountable to the highest standard of professional ethics.

Customer Service

We are committed to providing our customers with the highest quality and most cost-effective professional law enforcement service with the goal of enhancing the safety an quality of life within our community.

Empowerment

We are committed to the empowering of the members of our organization and the community to resolve problems by creating an environment that encourages solutions that address the needs of the community.

Fairness and Equality

We are committed to the delivery of police service that provides fair and equal treatment to all citizens and police personnel.

http://www.communitypolicing.org/planning/lewisville/values.html

ORGANIZATIONAL VALUES CHECKLIST*
AND WORKSHEET

____ Accessibility	____ Empowerment	____ Professionalism
____ Adaptability	____ Ethical Practice	____ Public Service
____ Appreciation	____ Excellence	____ Quality
____ Camaraderie	____ Expertise	____ Recognition
____ Change	____ Fairness	____ Resourcefulness
____ Communication	____ Fiscal Integrity	____ Respect
____ Compassion	____ Flexibility	____ Self Responsibility
____ Competence	____ Growth	____ Service
____ Competitiveness	____ Helping People	____ Stability
____ Cooperation	____ Honesty	____ Stewardship
____ Courtesy	____ Humanity	____ Team Spirit
____ Creativity	____ Initiative	____ Team Work
____ Customer Service	____ Integrity	____ Thoughtfulness
____ Democracy	____ Justice	____ Unity
____ Diversity	____ Listening	____ Value Staff
____ Effective Use of	____ Loyalty	
Resources	____ Mutual Respect	*Checklist adapted from a design by*
____ Effectiveness	____ Open Mindedness	*Charlotte Roberts in Senge, pg.210*

STEP # 1:

Read through the above list and identify the top ten values that you feel your organization should espouse.

STEP # 2:

Review your choices a second time and choose the five values that you think are the most important.

STEP # 3:

In the section below, write down your top five values in order of importance for the organization and briefly describe what each one means for you.

VALUE	MEANING FOR ME	RANK
		1
		2
		3
		4
		5

Alan D. Goodman, MSW, CSW

Alan Goodman has one of the most charming voices I've ever heard. He still has a slight accent from his birthplace, Johannesburg but there is something else in his accent. It probably has something to do with his six years living in Israel. I'm sure one of the reasons why his consulting clients adored him was his calm, relaxed manner.

Alan began his professional career in Israel working in a youth village with children from all over the world. He was the only social worker in a youth village and school of 700 kids from diverse cultures and economic backgrounds. He loved working with the children, watching them grow and change in response to their new learning environment. Many of the life lessons learned from these children in transition, he has been able to apply to his consulting practice.

Alan later worked as a field psychologist with the Israeli Army and finished up his service as a combat soldier in an artillery unit on the northern border. In Israel, he met his wife and soul mate, Susan, a consultant in records and information management from Queens, NY. They are really, really married: once in the States and a second time in Israel.

Alan and Susan moved to the United States in 1976. Alan received his MSW at Yeshiva University in NY, while holding down several part time jobs to pay the bills. For most of his professional career Alan has served as the executive director of social service and community service agencies within the Jewish community in Albany, NY and Detroit Michigan.

After returning to New York and continuing work in the Jewish communal field, Alan opened his own consulting firm, specializing in management consulting for the not for profit sector. Post 9/11, The American Red Cross in Greater New York heard about Alan and recruited him to head up the September 11 Recovery Program.

When not cleaning up disasters, Alan is working on a book on spiritual growth and awareness. He also has a small healing practice. Alan and Susan have a son and two daughters. Their son Adam is a researcher at E Entertainment Television, their daughter Shara works at Premier Radio in New York City and their youngest Taryn is a student at Evergreen State College in Olympia, Washington.

Alan Goodman, MSW, CSW
233 Soundview Avenue
White Planes, NY 10606
914-684-0313
E-mail: dart64@aol.com

CHAPTER 9

Strategic Decision-Making: Bringing Line Staff, Management and Board Together

Seymour J. Friedland, Ph.D.
and
Susan E. Mundry, Ed.M.

I. Introduction

In recent years, nonprofit organizations, like their for-profit counterparts, have seen the necessity for long-term planning and for staff engagement in strategic thinking. In fact, the completion of a strategic plan is one of the most serious obligations a group's board and management face. Typically, the management presents a draft plan, which is then revised by a board committee. Or the original draft may be a product of a joint board-management committee. Once the board approves the plan, it is disseminated to the staff – in some cases only to senior managers, in others to everyone who works for the organization. It is not unusual for individuals who have not been a part of a drafting committee to have little or no idea of the content, basic assumptions and issues that were important in its preparation. Yet they are asked to carry out the plan. In fact, many organizations maintain a type of "secrecy" about the strategic plan, sometimes even after its completion.

Although what we have described is typical, it is not particularly sensible. The successful implementation of a strategic plan requires the involvement of almost everyone in an organization, and often key stakeholders outside the organization. Individuals at every level have to support the goals and need to understand the underlying issues and assumptions of the plan if they are to later implement it successfully. This suggests that every individual in an organization should play some role in preparing a strategic plan. So why is it that this rarely happens? People usually give a variety of answers, such as the following:

- It is impractical and expensive to involve everyone.

- People at different levels in an organization vary greatly in their understanding and knowledge.

- Strategic planning is a very abstract, sophisticated process that is hard to reduce to a few simple steps.

- Individuals at various levels of a hierarchy have different perspectives, and it is hard to bring these together.

- People in less senior positions have less information and perspective to offer on future goals and organizational direction.

However, if an organization is going to take a really inclusive approach – and if it truly wants the ultimate buy-in of everyone – it must meet these challenges. The use of a *strategic-planning fair*, a type of retreat explained in this chapter, solves many of these problems. It enables an organization in the strategic-planning process to be inclusive, bringing people together from very different levels of authority, knowledge and understanding. The fair takes the abstract process of strategic planning and puts it in a more concrete form. It provides genuine decision-making activities so that what is frequently an intellectual exercise becomes more real. Most important, it creates a level playing field for all participants so that there is a genuine sense of being part of a team that includes all stakeholders: board, management and staff. This approach should result in enhanced and quicker buy-in of the completed strategic plan and a greater likelihood of achieving the goals of the planning process.

II. The Process

This section describes the actual steps of a *strategic-planning fair*, based on our own experience. Use these steps as a guideline, and tailor them to create a strategic planning fair for your own organization.

STEP 1. CHOOSING THE STRATEGIC AREAS

In *strategic-planning fairs*, participants focus on a limited number of key strategic areas that face the organization. But before this number is narrowed down, it is useful to gather as many strategic issues as possible. Here are some examples of strategic areas or issues: Where should we locate our offices to optimize services to our clients? What populations could we serve that we are currently not serving? Should we eliminate some of the services we provide? Are there services we are not offering that our clients want? Should we look for another organization with which to merge to expand our services or populations served?

An easy way to gather such issues is through a simple questionnaire that asks staff and clients to identify populations that need service, as well as services that are currently unavailable or of poor quality. Strategic areas can also be gathered at ongoing meetings, such as those of board committees, the senior management team, "town meetings," and program meetings. Simply ask: "What are our areas for growth and why?" and "Where should we eliminate services and why?"

We suggest that you identify at least three strategic areas, but no more than six, that are raised often by staff and clients in the know. The areas identified should:

- Show a direct connection to the organization's mission.

- Have an impact on quality.

- Involve a long-range time horizon.

- Relate to the organization's financial health.

Once you have chosen the critical strategic areas on which to focus, you are ready to design a strategic planning fair. Appoint a staff or board committee, or a blend of the two, to serve as the planners. It is good to have the committee chaired by a senior staff official or a board member to ensure that the resources needed are provided. The committee will be responsible for gathering and analyzing data and for preparing background materials.

STEP 2. ORGANIZE THE STRATEGIC-PLANNING FAIR AROUND STRATEGIC AREAS

The *strategic-planning fair* committee gathers and reviews data on each strategic area to frame the primary choices available to the organization. For example, in the strategic area addressing who the organization's clients should be, our committee considered who the agency presently served and in what ways, as well as the populations not being served. As an agency that had long been funded to provide services to the poor, a decision we faced was whether and how to market services privately to more affluent clients who were currently served by only a handful of the organization's programs. The committee identified this as a strategic decision to make. But before we could decide, we needed to know more about it. The committee members prepared an overview of the strategic area, gathered information that might affect our choices and then developed questions to guide the discussion. These included: What are the advantages and disadvantages of increasing our services for private pay clients? What would we need to do differently? Would the same services work for both populations?

It is this background thinking and framing that we think makes the *strategic-planning fair* so useful. When planning a fair, the committee examines each strategic area and lists the decisions needed for each. This information is then summarized in an information packet that is the focus of the *strategic-planning fair* discussion. The packet lists each strategic area the organization is focusing on, summarizes the key facts influencing each area, and portrays the three to five most important dilemmas or decisions points the organization is facing in this area.

Strategic Planning Fair Information Packet

I.   Strategic Area

II. Facts Influencing the Area

III. Strategic Dilemmas and Decisions

STEP 3. RESEARCH THE STRATEGIC AREAS

One of the major flaws of many strategic-planning processes is that they are "data-free." Seasoned professionals often believe they have enough information about their organizations and the fields they operate in to generate and make strategic choices. But in today's rapidly changing world this is not the case. Old assumptions need to be reviewed, and factual information should be the basis of decisions.

That is why the *strategic-planning fair* involves gathering factual material. These facts might include the size of certain populations in the service area, socioeconomic information, data on services purchased, types of competitors, and background on funding for each of the strategic areas. Ask yourselves: What do we know and what do we need to know about this strategic area to make good decisions?

In gathering this information you may want to use a variety of methods. One method uses focus groups led by professional facilitators and attended by the types of people your organization seeks to serve, as well as leaders from your field. Focus groups provide important data about client and funding needs and about competitors. Your committee can also gather data from staff through a questionnaire, and it can collect demographic information and service data from records. The Internet can be used to track many pieces of information – for example, census data. Simple questions, such as how many phone calls do you receive asking for certain services in one month versus another, provide useful data. The committee should also review the priorities and requirements of funding sources, such as philanthropies and public grants that fund the services within the strategic areas addressed.

The data gathered help to pinpoint the particular questions and choices you need to address within each strategic area. For example, through our process we learned that many of the organization's poorer clients had shifted from needing temporary assistance to being in a state of permanent poverty. This suggested that we develop and find funding for longer-term services and attack difficult problems, such as affordable housing. This decision point would not have emerged without a careful review of client and service information.

STEP 4. CREATING THE STRATEGIC DILEMMAS

What makes the *strategic-planning fair* unique is the use of "strategic dilemmas," or decision points, that the organization must address in each strategic area. Strategic dilemmas are stories or scenarios that depict in concrete form the issues that require decision-making. They are in a sense "dramatizations" of the key strategic questions. They should use "characters" that closely resemble the organization's clients and a setting that is familiar. The questions that each dilemma poses force the participants to make decisions that point to an underlying strategy. The dilemmas need to be well-written, interesting and vivid enough to capture the imagination and attention of participants. They should be about real people in real situations and, therefore, compelling examples of what a true decision is like. The strategic dilemmas, along with the factual information gathered, are compiled into an information packet that is distributed to everyone at the *strategic-planning fair*. (See example at the end of the chapter.)

STEP 5. PREPARING THE FACILITATOR

With your strategic areas identified, facts and data compiled, and strategic dilemmas written, you are ready to work with the facilitators who will guide the staff and board discussions during the fair. The fair is designed so that participants meet in small groups conducive to full participation and serious discussion. We recommend that you recruit professional facilitators to lead the small groups. This will maximize the effectiveness of the fair. In our case, we recruited highly skilled facilitators from business and industry in our area who agreed to provide the service free of charge.

At the facilitators' orientation, walk through the design for the small group meetings and ask the facilitators for suggestions for fine-tuning the process. Ask each one to practice by leading the rest of the group through a small part of the session. This will give them a chance to model for one another and you a chance to make sure that all have the skills needed to be effective. The greatest value of bringing the facilitators together is that they have the opportunity to clarify the intended outcomes of the session. They can plan ways to help the participants engage with the strategic areas, consider the facts and decision points and reach consensus on their recommendations. Make sure the facilitators understand why you have chosen particular strategic areas and what they mean – they may need to clarify this information for the staff and board members in their small groups.

STEP 6. INVITATION TO STAFF AND BOARD MEMBERS

The *strategic-planning fair* is intended as a very inclusive process. All staff and board members are invited and encouraged to attend. To increase participation, event planners can reach out to particular people to ask them to participate in the discussion of a specific strategic area. A simple note or e-mail saying, "We really hope to get your input on this area," goes a long way toward increasing participation. Telling staff that there will be many more opportunities for input can actually reduce participation, because staff members may think they can provide their ideas later. You need to remind people that there will be other times to engage with the strategic plan but that if they wish to influence what is *in* the plan, they need to be at the fair.

STEP 7. FOLLOW-UP

Strategic-planning events are often just that – events – when they are over, there is no follow-through. The fair is quite different. Through recordkeeping and reporting, staff members continue to engage in the strategic-planning process. During the small-group sessions the facilitators take detailed notes to document the suggestions and decisions of the group. These notes are later combined into a report summarizing the priorities for each of the strategic areas. Senior staff members then hold "town meetings" of all staff to get more insight into the actions the organization needs to take in each area. At that point they may assign responsibility to staff to take the next steps. All staff members continue to collect and review data to assess progress and plan next steps.

III. The Nuts and Bolts of a Strategic-planning Fair

1. **The physical setting** – Choose a site that has a large enough room for everyone to gather. There should be enough breakout rooms, of sufficient size and number, to accommodate the groups discussing strategic areas.

2. **Materials** – Each breakout room should be equipped with the following materials:

   - Tables for groups of four
   - Chart paper and markers
   - Information packets
   - Stations around the room with chart paper and markers
   - 3-by-5-inch Post-its

3. **The schedule** – Plan on about five hours for the fair. We suggest starting in late afternoon with a break for supper. The addition of food always creates a warmer atmosphere. Allow enough initial time for people to network, get to know one another informally and relax. There should be a welcome by a key figure in the organization, followed by a "framing" talk by either the board president or the CEO. The purpose of this presentation is to inspire participants, to lay out a vision and to set out important goals for the fair. This talk is really a call to action.

   If you are dealing with many issues and people, it is best to have two sets of concurrent sessions. That is, each person would participate in two consecutive groups dealing with two different issues. Each group would meet for two hours. If you are doing two sets of groups, it is important to break up the time between sessions with supper or some other refreshment.

The fair ends with a wrap-up. This is an opportunity to recognize those who helped create the fair, to thank participants, and to pledge to carry out the next steps.

4. **The Breakout Groups** – Try to have no more than 15 people in each group.

    A. The Packet (See sample at end of chapter) – Each participant in the group receives a packet for that strategic area that includes:

    *   An overview statement about the area.
    *   A fact Sheet that includes demographics, financial information, national and local trends.
    *   Strategic dilemmas – stories and vignettes about the strategic area that pose a question that participants must decide.

    B. Facilitators – Each facilitator should attend training before the fair to prepare him/her for the following format:

    *   Welcome, overview of the goals and agenda (5 minutes).
    *   Problems and dilemmas: Making meaning from staff and client experiences, data from the field and environmental factors (50 minutes).
    *   Implications and questions raised by the data (40 minutes).
    *   Issues for further action, reflection and dialogue (25 minutes).

    The group is encouraged to:

    *   Use all of the information provided and discuss how it affects the organization, its work, its clients, its funding and other aspects.
    *   Record insights and conclusions on chart paper and individual Post-its.
    *   Make real decisions about each dilemma for which there is some consensus.
    *   Describe new insights raised by the facts and dilemmas.

Each facilitator provides a write-up after the fair that includes the following: a summary of the process, decisions made by the group for each dilemma, information and assumptions used in making the decisions, and insights and opinions that were evident.

IV. Conclusion

Organizations can derive substantial benefits from using the *strategic-planning fair*. The process focuses all constituencies on the same areas and provides a data-driven rationale for why these areas are important to the organization. At the same time it introduces reality into the planning process by looking at how decisions would affect real clients and services. The process results in decisions that are easier to understand and act on because they are well-researched and defined. It enhances community participation in the final actions because members of the community have had a hand in shaping them, and it builds a greater understanding of why the organization is doing what it is doing. The process is ideal for helping staff members and other constituents build a shared vision of the future they desire and ideas for getting there.

These benefits are not realized without costs, however. The process is more time-consuming than the traditional forms of strategic planning that involve senior management only. A staff and board committee is needed, and all staff participate in at least one meeting. In addition, in our case, the program director devoted about 15 percent of his time over three to four months to plan, organize data collection and carry out the fair. We also invested in an outside consultant to help with the process and provide an external perspective. If you are interested in using a *strategic-planning fair*, we recommend that you give the staff the time needed to make it successful.

If you want to achieve the kinds of benefits we have, try this innovative approach to making decisions for your organization. The process works well for organizations of all types and sizes, especially in the nonprofit sector, where it is important to involve many stakeholders. It has moved us forward faster and with a better shared understanding than ever before. Staff and board members are talking with one another, engaged and energized. Most importantly, they know where the organization is going and are taking action to get us there.

V: Strategic-planning Fair
Sample Information Packet

This section provides a sample from an information packet used in our *strategic-planning fair*. The packet includes an *Overview* that frames the strategic area of focus, *Facts* that provide the data to inform decision-making, and *Strategic Dilemmas* that chronicle how decisions affect real clients and services.

STRATEGIC AREA: SENIOR SERVICES

OVERVIEW:

Everytown Service System (ESS) has developed comprehensive services for seniors. As America ages, the demand for senior services will continue to grow. The situation is complicated by the fact that federal support for these services has been decreased. On the other hand, this is probably the most affluent elderly generation that America has ever seen. There are many agencies competing for a share of the senior market. We must be flexible enough to adjust our services as regulations, reimbursement and our competitors change.

The agency is committed to serving seniors. That is a given. The important strategic questions that must be addressed are as follows:

How should we respond to the growing demand for services? What part of the "senior market" will be the focus of our services?

How do we position ourselves to be truly competitive in the future?

FACTS:

People are living longer than ever before. Currently, one in eight Americans is over 65 years old. By 2050, it is expected that one in five Americans will be over 65. Most dramatic is the increase in the oldest segment of society, those needing the most care. The "oldest-old" – those aged 85 and over – numbered 3 million in 1994, making them 10 percent of the elderly and 1 percent of the total population. In 2050, the "oldest-old" will number 19 million, making them 24 percent of elderly Americans and 5 percent of all Americans.

The elderly population in the United States is growing rapidly due to the aging of the baby boom generation and an increase in life expectancy. Life expectancy in the United States is now 76 years. Women live longer than men so that by age 85, there are five women for every two men. Providing services to the elderly means primarily serving women.

Seventy-five percent of noninstitutionalized elderly men live with a spouse, compared with only 41 percent of elderly women. Half of noninstitutionalized women over 85 years old live alone. This means that elderly women will often be without a spouse's help when they develop health problems.

Fifty percent of those over age 85 living in the community need help performing everyday tasks such as bathing, dressing and preparing meals. Family members provide most of the care for these seniors. The typical caregiver is 57, female, married and employed outside the home.

Nursing homes are an unpopular choice for senior adults. Nevertheless, 43 percent of today's seniors are expected to use a nursing home in their lifetime. Eighty-nine percent of those over 75 years old agree with the statement "I'd like to stay in my own home and never move." A growing popular choice for seniors is assisted living. Assisted living offers private rooms, meals and supervision. Even though the cost for assisted living is between $2,000 and $5,000 per month, 100 new assisted-living facilities were built in our state in the last five years.

The median income for elderly people doubled between 1957 and 1992. Today, the elderly as a group are better off than other Americans. The poverty rate is 15 percent for those under age 65 and only 11 percent for 65- to 74-year-olds. However, income disparities persist among various elderly subgroups. For example, white men have the highest median income, more than double that of elderly African-American women or Hispanic women.

At ESS, our Home Health, Homecare and Geriatric Mental Health programs focus on the frail elderly living in the community. The average age of our clients is 80, and 75 percent are women.

Fifty percent of all ESS clients are over age 65. At any one time, Geriatric Mental Health has a caseload of 200 clients, Homecare has 1,000, Home Health has 175. Our Guardianship program serves more than 30 wards, and the Long-term Care Ombudsman program surveys more than 40 nursing homes each month. These programs depend upon reimbursement from various governmental sources. Mental Health and Home Health receive reimbursement from Medicare and Medicaid. Homecare, Guardianship and Ombudsman depend upon state contracts. Only 15 percent of homemaker visits are private-pay.

Medicare reimburses Home Health services. The level of reimbursement has decreased significantly in the last few years, moving from fee-for-service to a "capitated" model. Documentation requirements have also been increased due to allegations of fraud in the home health industry. Twenty percent of home health agencies in our state have closed since 1996. Fortunately, our own Home Health program completed this past fiscal year with a small surplus.

* Facts from the U.S. Census Bureau and the 1995 CJP demographic survey report

STRATEGIC DILEMMAS:

ESS has developed an excellent reputation as a provider of senior services. We are well-positioned to grow in response to increasing demand, but this is a very competitive area. While we are deeply committed to building our senior services, we must make the right decisions now to continue to remain competitive and thrive in the future.

1. Mrs. Gold is a 75-year-old woman, living alone in a luxury apartment in an affluent suburb. She hears from a friend that ESS has high-quality homemaker services. She is interested in receiving services for herself from our agency. When she calls our Homecare department, she requests a homemaker for only

certain hours on Friday afternoons and expects the worker to be skilled in preparing Sabbath dinner. She is willing to pay privately for this service.

In order to accommodate Mrs. Gold, we would have to adjust our current procedures, set aside specific resources and provide special training to take on this assignment. Should we help her? In the future, should the agency develop more of such programs to attract affluent clients?

2. A 70-year-old man with a terminal illness calls our Healing program for advice. He has just been discharged from the hospital and will receive home health services. The discharge social worker in the hospital highly recommended a home health agency that will provide him with "everything he needs" as his illness worsens. It is a for-profit home health company that offers many extras in order to attract patients right out of the hospital. He would like services from our agency, but wants to be sure that we will offer him the same level of care.

   How would we convince this patient to choose ESS? Should we compete with for-profit organizations that are aggressively trying to increase their market share? Should we make the major investment in marketing that would be needed?

3. ESS provides home health and mental health services to an 80-year-old man, Mr. Smith, who has diabetes and depression. Nurses, a psychiatric social worker and a geriatric psychiatrist all provide treatment to him in his own home. Soon he will be transitioned to our adult day health program. As the nurse discusses the treatment plan, Mrs. Smith, who is 70, asks what kind of support the agency can offer her. She is recently retired and now will have much more time on her hands.

   What are the issues raised by Mrs. Smith's request? Should we have specialized services for her just as we do for her husband? What new programs should we develop for people facing retirement, the "young-old," those under 80?

Seymour J. Friedland, Ph.D.

When you meet Sy Friedland, there are two conflicting desires: one is to pinch his cheeks because he is so cute, the other is to sit at his feet and just listen because he is so insightful.

Sy is the Executive Director of Jewish Family and Children's Service of Greater Boston, which serves 26,000 clients annually in Eastern Massachusetts and employs more than 400 people.

Before coming to the Jewish Family and Children's Service of Greater Boston nine years ago, he was a popular consultant working with a variety of nonprofits in organizational design, strategic planning and governance.

Sy received his doctorate in clinical psychology from Clark University. He is nationally known for his presentations on strategic planning and board development and has published extensively in textbooks and professional journals on a broad spectrum of topics.

Sy is a leader in the Jewish Social Services Professionals Association and has served as the national chair, board member and committee member. He is also actively involved with the Association of Jewish Family and Children's Agencies.

When seen with his two grandchildren in public, most people assume he is the dad rather than the granddad. Sy has two children in their thirties and two teenagers, all of which keeps him young and tired. Sy's wife, Carol Stoltz runs the children's section of an independent bookstore.

When not hanging out with family, working or consulting, Sy enjoys portrait photography, listening to jazz, and gourmet cooking.

Sy Friedland, Ph.D.
Jewish Family & Children's Service of Boston
31 New Chardon St.
Boston, MA 02114-4701
617-227-6641
E-mail: sfriedl@jfcsboston.org

Susan E. Mundry, Ed.M.

Susan Mundry is further proof of Newton's laws of motion. She is always in motion, running major projects at the national research and development firm, WestEd, leading professional meetings around the country, and writing books as well as having fun with her husband, kids and friends. She demonstrates Newton's third law that for every action there is a reaction by mobilizing people to be the best they can be through her leadership development work. Take action and have fun is her mantra.

Susan consults for nonprofit organizations, and educational and professional associations primarily in three areas: leadership, resource development, and staff training and development. She helps clients by asking the hard questions, analyzing needs, and building clients' capacity for continuous improvement and change. Her great love is helping people embrace change as a constant condition and prepare their organizations to adapt.

Susan is an accomplished group facilitator, always making learning fun and interactive. She is the co-developer of two highly-acclaimed simulation board games called *Making Change* and *Systems Thinking/Systems Changing*. The games simulate the challenges and pitfalls of leading change efforts and demonstrate what's needed to support successful change. Her games have been used all over the US and Canada and in several other countries and one has been translated into four different languages.

When Susan does slow down it's to enjoy time with her family and friends. She enjoys skiing, boating, and most of all cooking. If you stop by anytime there will be something wonderful cooking on the stove (as well as in her mind)!

Susan Mundry
Director, National Academy for Leadership/WestEd
280 Merrimac Street
Newburyport, MA 01950
978-465-9360
E-mail: smundry@wested.org

CHAPTER 10

T Minus
60 Minutes & Counting:
Moving Successfully from
Retreat to Reality

David LaGreca, MBA

Introduction

Whew! There is one hour to go before the end of your board's annual retreat. A lot of time, energy and resources have been spent to get to this point – and the board and senior staff are (check all that apply):

✓ Exhausted but energized. ❏

✓ Ready to leave and get back to family/leisure/work. ❏

✓ Dazed and confused. ❏

✓ Planning for a much-needed post-retreat vacation. ❏

✓ On the verge of a meltdown. ❏

✓ Glazed over and indifferent – the way they arrived. ❏

The board chair is speaking – but everyone's mind is on the parking lot and blasting out of here back to the real world. Suddenly, as the time is counting down, someone asks the question that stops the clock:

We have been together for two days, spent over $3,000 in food and materials and lodging – not to mention our time. Can someone outline the decisions we have made – and how we are going to get started when we get back to the reality of our organization's life?

It seems self-evident to mention that you are in trouble if no one can answer this question [or if there is no flip chart with the answer already outlined on it] by the time you are ready to leave. But in fact, many retreats end with the entire group breathing a collective sigh of relief and averse to seeing each other for at least a month. As the retreat draws to a close, however, your organization is most in need of <u>focused attention</u> from its board and staff leadership, and it is at this point when you are most in danger of having minds wander!

So, how do we plan our retreats to ensure a successful blast-off into the everyday world of programs and budgets? **How can we use the last hour of the retreat to help us move from discussion through decision to implementation?** The answer is not rocket science (sorry!) but rather clear-cut. Keeping the imagery of space travel, we need to:

...ensure that everyone is **on board** for the journey, we have a clear **flight plan**, and everyone understands the role of the **flight crew**.

Implementing plans developed during a retreat assumes that some decisions have been made.[1] So, if a board has followed the sage advice given by my fellow authors in the preceding chapters, your organization is facing the last hour of time with a series of decisions that need to be translated into action. Success in implementing these decisions is contingent on repeating and reiterating three basic rules:

---

[1] I believe that if there is nothing to decide at a regular board meeting, there is no need to meet. This goes doubly for retreats (See Chapter 4 in *The Secrets of Successful Boards*). Therefore, retreats where the ONLY purpose is bonding are of questionable value; try dinner or drinks after work instead.

1. **Make Sure Everyone Is on Board,** or at the least, make sure the key players are with you.

2. **Map Out the Flight Plan.** Make sure everyone understands where the organization is going.

3. **Identify the Flight Crew.** Let everyone know who is in charge of doing what, and when.

These rules are crucial to your organization moving successfully from your retreat experience back to the reality of your everyday organizational life. **Remember, the quality of your retreat is not measured just by the experience of your time together, but by the impact of the retreat on your organization's life.**

> ## Preflight Checklist #1
>
> Pay careful attention to the schedule of your retreat's last hour. At this time, you need to re-direct the energy of the group from discussion to action.
>
> The last hour should include a review and restatement of the issues:
>
> ✓ Decided, and
> ✓ Those still open for discussion and decision.
>
> This time should also include a broad overview of the post-retreat calendar, and identification of each individual responsible for implementation.
>
> Don't forget to say thank you – retreats are hard work and often above and beyond the call of duty.

1. Make Sure Everyone Is on Board

Retreats are a time when board members get to understand one another better, learn more about the organization and make decisions. When decisions have been made, some action must be taken after the retreat to implement them. It's critical to the success of any plan that everyone be on board concerning the decisions made. The more mission-critical the decisions, the more time will need to be spent on achieving buy-in from the organization's board and staff leadership.

If the retreat has been a success – and some fundamental aspects of the organization have been either re-affirmed or changed – there is a great deal of post-retreat work that needs to be done. It must be clear which board and staff members can be counted on as active and committed crew members.

Preflight Checklist #2

If you have name cards on the table during the retreat – the kind that stand up – place a small construction-paper rocket ship on each one with the person's first name on it.

At the last session, when the facilitator spells out the agreements, each participant that is supportive can paste his or her rocket on the flip chart.

A warning: some board and staff members may choose not to get on board. When the discussion focuses on major issues of importance to the organization, it is often evident when some member of the "crew" is withdrawing in disagreement. Time spent exploring such disagreements is useful and can determine the long-term success of your plans. However, while it is important to get buy-in, it is equally important to be realistic – and identify – disagreements:

> *For example, during its retreat, a 20 year-old organization devoted to giving preschool children a chance to enter school with better reading and social skills decides to establish a new program to share its experience with concerned educators in other states and countries. For one board member who has served for 10 years, this shift moves the organization away from what he perceives to be its original mission and he can't be supportive of the decision to expand the scope of the program. His heart lies with the local community, and he perceives the board as turning its back on local children.*

Remember: the more important the decision-making, the more impassioned the agreement to support it – and the decision to withhold support. The reality is that when mission-critical issues are made, some members of the board and staff may choose not to board the ship! We need to face such fundamental disagreements not as failures to communicate, but the natural decision of some to travel with us and others to take a different path.

Remember, implementation succeeds when everyone is on board!

2. Map Out the Flight Plan

Everyone is on board. Now, where are we going? And what are the stages of the journey we must undertake to make sure we get there?

Think of the work of the retreat as your Preflight Plan. The "work" of the retreat includes the results of all of the decisions made – with responsible individuals identified for each task, and a work calendar that shows the benchmarks along the trajectory of success. While the Flight Plan will

---

Preflight Checklist #3

Early space pioneers succeeded because they continually "pushed the envelope."

Successful planning requires some board members to constantly <u>push the envelope</u> and challenge themselves and the staff to ensure the plan stays on track.

---

guide your work as you end your retreat, the work done before and during the retreat is a major factor contributing to an implementation's success. While structuring the retreat discussions means that the outcomes will be structured as well, some additional things are crucial to reaching your destination:

1. **Successful implementation takes into account the boost a group gets from success.** So, when setting up your post-retreat flight plan, include an early win! If your organization has decided to embark on doubling the size of a program, for example, make the first stage of the project something doable. You will encounter enough bumpiness on the ride; do all you can to make the first leg of your journey a success.

2. **Aim for your own galaxy–not the next one!** Strategic plans that go into great detail about myriad things that "will" be accomplished without taking into account the basic constraints of the organization end up on shelves. Be realistic, detailed and assign time frames.

3. **Build in a schedule of "course corrections."** A good plan allows for a regular schedule of follow-up. Some of the best strategic decisions made in August 2001 may have been rendered meaningless by the events of September 11. If the

plan does not provide a mechanism for review and corrections, it is probably already forgotten, and your investment wasted.

In mapping out such a flight plan, an organization should be careful not to allow diversions to push it off track. Two common ones are:

"There is only ONE path":

Some organizations get tied up in endless discussions about how to implement a decision. The assumption here is that there is only one way to get from Point A to Point B:

If one of the strategic decisions is to pursue public funding for your organization's job-training program, there is a maddening array of programs to review. In addition to the fact that there are local, state and federal-level funding streams, each of these levels has multiple programs from which to choose. There is no one way to implement the board's decision. Research must be done before the organization can move forward – and decisions must be made.

"Lets take ANOTHER extravehicular walk":

Just as the board and staff are heading in one agreed-upon direction, some member of the team breaks away, and goes out on his own. This can be frustrating to the members of the team, particularly when everyone is under the impression that decisions have already been made and the Flight Plan is set. While the temptation is to try to shut the shuttle bay doors and leave the person lost in space, it may be necessary to reel in the individual before moving on. This is the role of the Flight Commander:

After a particularly long and difficult mission review at one board's retreat, a former board member responded negatively to a draft of a new mission statement. At the next board meeting, one board member tried to revisit two days of work. The members, patiently – and expediently – talked through the issues and brought the individual back on board.

3. Identify the Flight Crew

Everyone is on board and we know where we want to go, now, who can help us get there? Whose responsibility is it to implement the decisions made during the board retreat? The following two extreme cases of behavior illustrate the need to clarify the post-retreat roles of board and staff.

SCENARIO #1 – BOARD TO STAFF: TAKE CARE OF IT!

On the way to their cars, the board leadership hands the flip charts to the executive director and tells her to type them up and set the plans in motion. That could include anything from changing the organization's logo and stationery to starting a major new program initiative.

SCENARIO #2 – BOARD TO STAFF: WE'LL TAKE CARE OF IT!

On the way to their cars, the board leadership tells the executive director not to worry, "they will take care of it." This leads to two variations:

✓ The board does nothing – and the executive director spends the next two weeks trying to retrieve the flip charts from the back seat of a board member's car before they get destroyed and any record of the weekend disappears.

✓ The board leadership plunges ahead, making decisions on their own without communicating with other board members and the staff. In this scenario, reams of new stationery could arrive with no notice!

So, who is in charge? To ensure successful implementation of retreat decisions, several roles should be defined BEFORE everyone leaves the retreat.

Flight Commander: A board member is typically charged with monitoring the activities that resulted from the retreat (the Flight Plan). While this role may belong to the board chair, it is often better to ask another board member to manage this process. Upon leaving the retreat, the board chair is faced with the normal work of the board – nominations, audits, making sure committees do their work, partnering with the executive director, etc. The post-retreat Flight Commander needs to be able to coordinate the activities of all the board members and staff members that have assumed responsibility for some future action during the course of the retreat.

To assist the Flight Commander, it is a good idea to add several individuals to the crew's leadership team:

Program Specialist: The executive director's post-retreat role is to monitor any decisions made concerning the organization's program. Among the issues that might be overseen are the implementation of a program evaluation process, expansion of the organization's programs to a new population, or provision of a new service to the organization's traditional population.

Structural Engineer: A board member could be asked to oversee any decisions made concerning infrastructure issues. These issues might encompass a major fund-raising campaign such as a capital drive, board development, finding a new office, etc.

Communications Specialist: As changes begin to take place in your organization, it is necessary to keep everyone up to date on what is happening. A good way to do this is to link every change to a discussion/decision from the retreat. This specialist's work could begin with developing a briefing book of all the discussion and actions of the retreat for every attendee. This type of a document also serves as a crucial link to members of the board or staff who were unable to attend the retreat. As more retreat decisions are implemented, it will be important to develop creative ways to remind board and staff of milestones achieved and the journey ahead.

NOTE: These individuals do NOT do all the work! They have a coordinating/cajoling/motivating role in keeping the momentum of the retreat going. Nor are the descriptions meant to be restrictive. For example, it is clear that infrastructure issues concerning a capital drive or finding new office space must involve the executive director.

Prior to ending the retreat, these people should be recognized and their roles explained to the board and staff. As the Flight Crew their job will be to keep everyone (and everything) on track.

> ### Preflight Checklist #4
>
> There is a reason teachers use gold stars when correcting papers; the star announces something to everyone!
>
> Make badges with Flight Commander, Program Specialist, Structural Engineer and Communications Specialist on them, and award them to the your flight's leadership team!

Start Your Engines Now:
Pre-Departure Exercises & Tasks

It's time to blast off! Everyone is on board, the flight plan has been mapped out in detail and the Flight Crew is in place. Now, how can you ensure that you will successfully complete your journey back to organizational life?

1. **Debrief the group.**

   As the retreat draws to a close, **get participants focused on their role in the organization's past and future.** For example, the group can be asked to answer several questions such as:

   Celebration: Have participants share something they are celebrating in their personal, professional or volunteer life. Follow up by asking them to look forward to next year's retreat and answer the same question: What do they want to be celebrating a year from now?

   Try this on for size: Ask everyone to review the changes that have been discussed during the retreat, and to imagine their impact. As board and staff members, does this work still "fit" them personally? Are their skills and experiences still needed by the organization as it changes? Is the work of the organization still a match for each person's interests and beliefs? Is there a fit?

Reaffirmation: Ask each participant to take a few moments and then share an explicit connection between something that was discussed during the retreat and something the organization does day to day to achieve its mission. What about this connection reaffirms the work of volunteers and staff?

Stand by me: If there is a great deal of excitement generated by the work done during the retreat, this might be a good time to ask people to re-commit to their volunteer roles. You can ask participants what concrete actions they are ready to commit to over the next year (and make sure someone is taking notes so the communications specialist can share this information with everyone later).

2. **Reduce the plan to one page of bullet points.**

Take some time during the last hour of the retreat **to reduce your decisions to one page of bullet points.** Too many plans are too long! To be successful, everyone needs to understand the core decisions that have been made. That means the plan has to be short! In fact, a one-page plan, with quarterly updates of achievements is a great way to communicate to an organization's various stakeholders.

The plan should be broken down into the major areas of development needed:

✓ Program: expansion of existing programs and services, development of new ones, potential geographical expansion, etc.

✓ Organization: staff reorganization, upgrade of fiscal skills on staff, division of program staff to serve new geographical area, etc.

✓ Resource: outreach to new funders, a capital campaign, new fund-raising efforts, special events, etc.

✓ Board: expansion, training, restructuring, increased attendance, etc.

Each of these four areas could have several bullets that include the time frame for achievement and the responsible party. This is a real Flight Plan that has the potential to really get you somewhere!

3.   Build accountability into the process.

Review your decisions to see if **accountability is built into the process** as you move forward. The difference between just a plan and the successful implementation of organizational change is holding yourselves accountable for change.

As you near the end of the retreat, you need to begin to make explicit an accountability calendar. This calendar should cover at least one year, stating the responsible party for leading each task as well as when it is due. The calendar should be broken down into doable tasks. For a retreat that took place on the weekend of April 1, an appropriate entry might be:

Date: June 1

Who: Board Chair & Executive Director

What: Present to the board the results of three interviews with fund-raising firms that could assist in our capital campaign. If possible, make a recommendation to hire one of the firms.

The following type of accountability statement should be strenuously **avoided**:

Date: October 1

Who: The Board

What: Raise $1,000,000 for capital improvement of our facility.

4. **Continually remind your team of your decisions.**

    Discuss how your decisions and changes will be kept before the board and staff as you move ahead. It could be as easy as having a standing agenda item at each board, committee and staff meeting to allow for discussion of the status of each area of the plan. Or have the Communications Specialist develop a newsletter or Webpage to facilitate communication.

5. **Remember, it's a big universe out there.**

    Having initiated your organizational countdown – and blasted off – the journey may be quite intimidating to the crew. Several things should be kept in mind for times when things are less than clear:

    ✓ It's the mission! All of the planning, time, volunteer and staff energy in the universe cannot ensure success unless the organization stays true to its mission. The yardstick for measuring all planning activities is a simple one: Does this help further our mission?

    ✓ Not everything will succeed! Despite all your efforts, some of the original planning decisions will be unsuccessful. Or will grow and change into something you could not have imagined when you began. The trick is to keep your organization open to the change necessary to let organic things happen.

                    *   *   *   *   *

Finally, let's return to the original question asked by the retreat participant while everyone was mentally packing his or her bags an hour before the end of our retreat:

Can someone outline the decisions we have made—and how we are going to get started when we get back to the reality of our organization's life?

Your answer to this original question is a clear indication of whether your organization will have a successful journey back to its everyday world – and an almost limitless range of possible futures! Check to see if you have:

✓ Everyone on board.

✓ A succinct Flight Plan.

✓ The right Flight Crew.

Now, you are on your way: T-minus 60 minutes and counting....59....58....57...

David M. LaGreca, MBA

David LaGreca is still a man with a past – one that now includes his contributions to the *SECRETS OF SUCCESSFUL BOARDS* and the *SECRETS OF SUCCESSFUL FUNDRAISING*. In 1999, David established his own consulting practice – The LaGreca Company – assisting nonprofit and for-profit groups in managing change. His work focuses on board development, strategic planning and managing workplace operations.

Prior to 1999, David LaGreca spent eight years as a consultant at the Volunteer Consulting Group (VCG). His responsibilities included nonprofit board recruitment and consulting, meeting facilitation, the corporate placement program (American Express, PSE&G, Ernst & Young LLP), VCG's national initiatives and overall management of VCG's information systems.

Before joining VCG in 1991, Mr. LaGreca was the Administrator for the Department of Surgery, Memorial Sloan Kettering Cancer Center. He also taught at Boston College, wrote a weekly newspaper column in Rhode Island and has spent the last twenty years working with community-based health care organizations caring for terminal patients.

A graduate of the Katholieke Universiteit te Leuven, Belgium, Mr. LaGreca received his MBA from the Columbia University School of Business. As a former diocesan and Jesuit priest, he has worked with a wide variety of nonprofits addressing issues covering education, health care, homelessness, and human rights.

A native of Rhode Island, Mr. LaGreca has lived, worked and studied in Belgium, England, Germany, Italy, Jamaica, Massachusetts and Tanzania.

Mr. LaGreca served on the Boards of Hospice Care of Rhode Island and McAuley House (Providence, RI). He served as Chair of the Board of Body Positive of New York – a position he held for five years. He currently sits on the Board of Directors of the Vocational Foundation, Inc. and on the Advisory Board of the MBA-Nonprofit Connection.

David M. LaGreca
The LaGreca Company
4 West 104th Street, #LB, New York, NY 10025-4318
212-222-3892
E-mail: dmlnyc@aol.com

Feed your board for success, not coma!